PLANT SCIENCE RESEARCH AND PRACTICES

MARIJUANA

MEDICAL USES, REGULATIONS AND LEGAL ISSUES

PLANT SCIENCE RESEARCH AND PRACTICES

Additional books in this series can be found on Nova's website under the Series tab.

Additional e-books in this series can be found on Nova's website under the e-book tab.

PLANT SCIENCE RESEARCH AND PRACTICES

MARIJUANA

MEDICAL USES, REGULATIONS AND LEGAL ISSUES

MARGIE VASQUEZ
EDITOR

nova publishers
New York

Additional color graphics may be available in the e-book version of this book.

Library of Congress Cataloging-in-Publication Data

Names: Vasquez, Margie, editor.
Title: Marijuana : medical uses, regulations and legal issues / editor: Margie Vasquez.
Other titles: Plant science research and practices.
Description: Hauppauge, New York : Nova Science Publishers, [2016] | Series: Plant science research and practices | Includes index.
Identifiers: LCCN 2015048134 (print) | LCCN 2016000017 (ebook) | ISBN 9781634844093 (hardcover) | ISBN 9781634844246 ()
Subjects: LCSH: Marijuana--Therapeutic use. | Marijuana--Law and legislation.
Classification: LCC RM666.C266 M38 2016 (print) | LCC RM666.C266 (ebook) | DDC 362.29/55610973--dc23
LC record available at http://lccn.loc.gov/2015048134

Published by Nova Science Publishers, Inc. † New York

CONTENTS

PREFACE

Cannabis sativa is the scientific name for the widely used drug commonly known as marijuana. Marijuana is the most commonly used illegal drug in the United States as well as in many other countries. Considered a "soft" drug, it is a naturally growing plant that is harvested as its crude product for use. Other familiar names for marijuana are weed, dope, pot, hemp, cannabis, and reefer. Marijuana contains tetrahydrocannabinol (THC), which is a mind altering substance that is generally smoked, but also can be taken orally or as oil on the skin in order to receive a "high." New laws regarding the marijuana's legalization have led to more questions and increased interest in the effect marijuana has on its users. Chapter One of this book discusses differences across motivation variables and marijuana use. Chapter Two compares the medical necessity of marijuana to the political agenda. Chapter Three examines the evidence for and against the medical use of marijuana, and the effects and implications of its recent legalization in several states especially with regard to its use by college-age young adults. Chapter Four examines the issues surrounding legalization and teen use and the policy steps that might be taken to effectively communicate the risks to adolescents amidst an ever more socially acceptable climate. Chapter Five discusses the recent rise of legally sold marijuana, the risks of use, arguments in support of mandating warnings on packages of legally sold marijuana, the likely benefits and costs of mandating warnings, ways of evaluating proposed and actual warnings, and specific recommended warnings. Chapter Six exhibit how and the extent to which federal government marijuana regulation and policy contributes to disparities in arrest, in particular for African Americans of lower socioeconomic standing. This book ends with a commentary on aims to answer the question of whether marijuana and video games can engender "real" addictions in a way that bridges the gap between scientific and colloquial understandings of problem use.

Chapter 1 – *Cannabis sativa* is the scientific name for the widely used drug commonly known as marijuana. Tetrahydrocannabinol (THC) is the chemical that is responsible for the mind altering effects of Cannabis sativa; THC does this by binding to the Cannabinoid I Receptor (CB1) in the orbital frontal cortex – the area of the brain that controls motivation and emotion. New laws regarding the drug's legalization have led to more questions and increased interest in the effect marijuana has on its users. In the present study, participants (n = 195) ages 18 and older from around the United States completed online questionnaires regarding their demographics and marijuana use (Heavy, Occasional, Non) as well as two surveys – the Achievement Motivation Inventory (AMI) and Apathy Evaluation Scale (AES) – to measure motivation. There was no significant differences across the demographic variables and marijuana use. Also, in the AES and overall AMI there was no significant relationship between marijuana use and motivation. However, as there was a significant relationship between marijuana use and three of the individual categories of the AMI (Confidence in Success, Internality, Pride in Productivity).

Chapter 2 – Marijuana is classified by the Drug Enforcement Agency (DEA) as an illegal Schedule I drug which has no accepted medical use. However, recent studies have shown that medical marijuana is effective in controlling chronic non-cancer pain, alleviating nausea and vomiting associated with chemotherapy, treating wasting syndrome associated with AIDS, and controlling muscle spasms due to multiple sclerosis. These studies state that the alleviating benefits of marijuana outweigh the negative effects of the drug, and recommend that marijuana be administered to patients who have failed to respond to other therapies. Despite supporting evidence, the DEA refuses to reclassify marijuana as a Schedule II drug, which would allow physicians to prescribe marijuana to suffering patients. The use of medical marijuana has continued to gain support among states, and is currently legal in 23 states and the District of Columbia and Guam. This is in stark contrast to the federal government's stance of zero-tolerance, which has led to a heated legal debate in the United States. After reviewing relevant scientific data and grounding the issue ethically, there is a strong argument for allowing physicians to prescribe marijuana for medical purposes. Patients have a right to all beneficial treatments and to deny them this right violates their basic human rights.

Chapter 3 – The use of marijuana has been a controversial issue since the early 20th century when regulation and restriction on its use began to take hold, culminating in its classification as a Schedule I controlled substance under the 1970 Comprehensive Drug Abuse Prevention and Control Act (Controlled Substances Act), and hence its prohibition in the United States. However, studies on marijuana have shown some evidence for beneficial medical use of the substance. These medical uses include the treatment of acute and chronic pain, symptomatic relief in AIDS, and treatment of cancer, mental illness and addiction among others. Nevertheless marijuana, like numerous other pharmacologic substances, has its documented adverse effects including hallucinations, short-term memory and learning deficits, loss of coordination, increased risk of respiratory tract and other cancers, and increased tendency to use other dangerous and addictive substances such as cocaine. Furthermore, there have been major concerns expressed by opponents over the state-level legalization of medical marijuana with the view that legalization will make the drug more appealing and readily accessible to young adults (college-age students), thereby worsening the existing public health problem. This review of literature examines the evidence for and against the medical use of marijuana, and the effects and implications of its recent legalization in several states especially with regard to its use by college-age young adults. The findings of this review will provide information that will have the potential to contribute to the development of policies that will better protect the health and well-being of college students and allow for the development of prevention messages and interventions to serve this vulnerable group.

Chapter 4 – In the past decade, Americans have seen public opinion towards marijuana shift from a majority opposed to a majority in favor of making the substance legal for recreational use. Despite federal laws maintaining a strict prohibition of marijuana as a schedule 1 drug, nearly half of all states have legalized marijuana for medical use, while others have taken the unprecedented step of legalizing marijuana for recreational use as well. However, due to the federal restriction on funds for marijuana research, evidence for the long term effects of marijuana use is lacking. The limited research that does exist concerning the effects of marijuana on children is as diverse and conflicted as drug policy itself, with some studies suggesting a risk of permanent cognitive impairment, while others find no linkage between adolescent marijuana use and physical or mental health problems in adulthood. Issues of commercialization juxtaposed against similarities and differences to tobacco and alcohol are at the forefront of concerns surrounding the impact on adolescent use. Policy makers must consider how evolving laws and social norms may affect adolescent experimentation and uptake. This commentary will examine the issues surrounding legalization and teen use and the policy steps that might be taken to effectively communicate the risks to adolescents amidst an ever more socially acceptable climate.

Chapter 5 – This chapter covers the recent rise of legally sold marijuana, the risks of marijuana use, arguments in support of mandating warnings on packages of legally sold marijuana, the likely benefits and costs of mandating warnings, ways of evaluating proposed and actual warnings, and specific recommended warnings. The chapter also describes a court-imposed duty to warn as a possible alternative to legislatively or administratively-mandated warnings.

Chapter 6 – The intent of this review is to exhibit how and the extent to which federal government marijuana regulation and policy contributes to disparities in arrest, in particular for African Americans of lower socioeconomic standing, thus leading to other negative outcomes including but not limited to poverty, health disparities, increased rates of sexually transmitted infections (STIs) and substance use and abuse. In this discussion, the authors will focus on the political history that has been institutionally imbued in the American politics and criminal justice system that increases the likelihood that African Americans, especially males, will be linked to stereotypical stigma that is a function of Western culture's socialization of men to accept norms that are not defined by the subjective experiences of African Americans. In conclusion, the authors proffer implications for perspective solutions to this problem including enhancing the quality of educational institutions and reducing educational failure in elementary and high schools, investments to enrich the quality of neighborhood environments and changes in policing and criminal justice policy that targets disproportionally African Americans, the poor and minorities.

Chapter 7 – What recreational marijuana use and entertainment video game play have in common is that they are benign much of the time, but they also have problem use patterns associated with them, and these problem use patterns are often misunderstood by both users and people concerned about them. One example of this misunderstanding is the question of whether marijuana and video games can engender "real" addictions. This commentary aims to answer this question in a way that bridges the gap between scientific and colloquial understandings of problem use, in hopes of helping service providers communicate effectively with users about whether they have a problem.

In: Marijuana
Editor: Margie Vasquez
ISBN: 978-1-63484-409-3

Chapter 1

MARIJUANA AND MOTIVATION

Larissa Reck and F. Richard Ferraro [*]
University of North Dakota, Grand Forks, ND, US

ABSTRACT

Cannabis sativa is the scientific name for the widely used drug commonly known as marijuana. Tetrahydrocannabinol (THC) is the chemical that is responsible for the mind altering effects of Cannabis sativa; THC does this by binding to the Cannabinoid I Receptor (CB1) in the orbital frontal cortex – the area of the brain that controls motivation and emotion. New laws regarding the drug's legalization have led to more questions and increased interest in the effect marijuana has on its users. In the present study, participants (n = 195) ages 18 and older from around the United States completed online questionnaires regarding their demographics and marijuana use (Heavy, Occasional, Non) as well as two surveys – the Achievement Motivation Inventory (AMI) and Apathy Evaluation Scale (AES) – to measure motivation. There was no significant differences across the demographic variables and marijuana use. Also, in the AES and overall AMI there was no significant relationship between marijuana use and motivation. However, as there was a significant relationship between marijuana use and three of the individual categories of the AMI (Confidence in Success, Internality, Pride in Productivity).

[*] Corresponding author: F. R. Ferraro, Dept. Psychology, Univ. North Dakota Stop 8380 Grand Forks, ND 58202, 701-777-2414 f.richard.ferraro@email.und.edu.

Keywords: marijuana, motivation, college students

MARIJUANA AND MOTIVATION

Marijuana is the most commonly used illegal drug in the United States as well as in many other countries (Justinova, Goldberg, Heishman, & Tanda, 2005). Considered a "soft" drug, it is a naturally growing plant that is harvested as its crude product for use. Other familiar names for marijuana are weed, dope, pot, hemp, cannabis, and reefer. Marijuana contains tetrahydrocannabinol (THC), which is a mind altering substance that is generally smoked, but also can be taken orally or as oil on the skin in order to receive a "high." The "high" associated with marijuana is characterized by users as a relaxed, euphoric feeling. Through many studies, it has been found that casual and daily use of the drug can alter brain structure and function, particularly in the areas involved in motivation and emotion. America's youth has a particularly alarming view of the dangers of the drug, with 60 percent of high school seniors believing that marijuana is not dangerous (Madras, 2014).

In the 1839, medicinal use of marijuana was first introduced by a British physician into Western medicine. The desired properties of marijuana were that it was a sedative and analgesic. For the next few years, marijuana was used to treat a variety of ailments, including rheumatism and convulsions in infants. At the time, there were no known detrimental side effects of marijuana and its somewhat weaker effects made it very attractive to physicians. Marijuana was widely used medicinally and recreationally in America until 1937, when the Marijuana Tax Act was passed. This law taxed marijuana for sale in attempt to slow its industrial growth. At this time in U.S. history, marijuana was not a widely used substance. Not until 1970, did the government place laws prohibiting marijuana (Mikuriya, 1969).

Cannabis sativa is incredibly complex with over 480 known compounds contributing to its chemical make-up (ElSholy & Slade, 2005). Unlike other drugs such as heroin, cocaine, and alcohol, marijuana is not usually a purified drug when used recreationally; it is taken directly from nature as a crude product and used (Dupont, 1997). THC is the main desired psychoactive chemical identified in the marijuana plant, however there are numerous other cannabinoids that cause symptoms in the user. Cannabis plants can be grown in different forms, which all differ in the amount of THC present (Goldstein, 2001).

While in the brain, THC starts to produce a "high" or altered state of thinking. There is a specific receptor for THC in the brain that has been identified called CB1, cannabinoid receptor. High concentrations of CB1 receptors are found in the hippocampus, nucleus accumbens, amygdala, and cerebral cortex. These areas are responsible for changes in mood and perception (Goldstein, 2001). When the receptor is activated, the release of amino acid and monoamine neurotransmitters are inhibited. This results in depolarization-induced suppression of inhibition or excitation in the hippocampus and cerebellum (Iverson, 2003). In experiments where the CB1 receptor was removed from the brain, there was no sign of reward or pleasure stimulation from THC, as well as reduced effects by morphine and other opiates (Goldstein, 2001). Marijuana is a very interesting drug because it is thought to work on the brain's reward pathway, but only in limited doses. At high doses, marijuana has adverse effects such as paranoia that counteract the brain's reward pathway (Justinova et al., 2005).

Cannabinoids increase the firing of dopamine (DA) neurotransmitters and leads to more dopamine being present in certain pathways. New discovery of the interaction between the two pathways has lead scientists to look the Cannabinoid receptor type 1 (CB1) for treatment of dopamine-related neuropsychological disorders. Using CB1 antagonists could have an impact on the firing of DA neurotransmitters and offer some insight on other ways to treat illnesses (Khoury et al., 2012).

Contrary to other research, Fibley et al., found stronger connectivity in the brains of marijuana users. Recruited were 48 users of marijuana were age and sex matched with 62 non users that acted as the control. MRI was used to measure participants' gray matter throughout the whole brain, functional connectivity among synapses, and structural connectivity in the white matter. Similar to other marijuana research, decreased gray matter was found in the frontal cortex of the brains of the drug users compared to the gray matter found in non-users' brains. However, higher functional and structural connectivity were found in the same areas that were lacking in matter. The significance of these findings is that it suggests that the brain may be able to adapt to the presence of marijuana – allowing it to work as effectively as the brain of a non-user even though less gray matter is present.

Marijuana has a noticeable effect on behavior in small doses. Short term use has less devastating long-term effects; however, it still can do considerable damage. When a person is high on marijuana everything is in slow motion. Short-term memory is disrupted, reaction time and learning is slowed, and perception of time and space is distorted. Often times, the person experiencing the high may be amused by little things or emotionless to certain stimuli. It is almost like they are in some sort of a trance (Dupont, 1997). When high, people often feel unusual emotional sensitivity, making them feel closer to others. Often times, people report increased sexual pleasure; however, it is hard to determine if it is in their altered state of mind that it's more pleasurable or if it's actually more pleasurable (Goldstein, 2001). In excessive amounts, marijuana can produce adverse effects such a paranoia, panic, anxiety, and almost schizophrenic-like symptoms.

Stereotypical seasoned marijuana users are often known as lazy and careless. In the most extreme cases, drug abusers may be diagnosed with amotivational syndrome, resulting in lack of motivation, empathy, drive, and care. These people suffer from this all the time, not just while high. Drug abusers often refer to this stage as "burnout," and it is seen in many different drugs of abuse. Marijuana works in a much slower way than other common drugs such as cocaine, however, and can stunt a person's personal growth, self-improvement, and self-worth (Dupont, 1997).

Although marijuana addiction is similar to other substance addiction such as nicotine, alcohol, and cocaine, it is thought to be slightly less severe. Marijuana addiction is the most commonly seen illicit drug addiction, not because it's addictive properties are so strong, but rather because it is much more commonly used than other illicit drugs such as heroin or cocaine. Usually, a user is considered addicted after ten years of daily use with six or more attempts to quit (Budney et al., 2007). Characterization of marijuana addiction is much more lenient than that of other drugs such as cocaine or even alcohol. Marijuana addicts continue use of the drug in all circumstances, no matter the negative side effects it may have. Family problems, job jeopardy, and social rejection are not enough to stop the addicted from using the drug. Some addicts even report withdrawal symptoms when they try to quit.

A large majority of the patients placed in treatment for marijuana addiction are under 25 years old. Many of these young people are also associated with trouble with the law and unproductivity. It is undetermined whether this is as a result of marijuana use or if the risk taking behavior leads to the addiction (Budney et al., 2007).

Marijuana is currently a topic of hot political debate in the United States. In 2014, Washington and Colorado legalized recreational marijuana use for those 21 years and older. Oregon and Alaska will be joining them in 2016. Twenty-seven states have legalized marijuana for medical use or decriminalized the substance. Decriminalization just reduces the penalties that were previously associated with the drug (Boyette & Wilson, 2015).

Previous research has been done on the amotivational syndrome with a variety of different methods and results. One such research was performed in a European city involved 238 student athletes from a large independent sports training facility with majors such as education, coaching, or athletic training. Although numerous nationalities were represented in the subject pool, all of the subjects were exceptional athletes that had spent much of their lives working to achieve their athletic goals. The subjects were asked to voluntarily complete Halikas et al.,'s criterion question for amotivational syndrome and a questionnaire involving marijuana use (1982). The results found that there was not really any consistencies between marijuana use and the amotivational syndrome as measured by the particular questionnaire used. In this study, researchers said that possibly their approach to assessing the amotivational syndrome were possibly to simplistic or else there is really no correlation between lack of motivation and marijuana use.

Another study was done looking at motivation, life satisfaction, and marijuana use. In this study, researchers only had two groups of users – those who used every day and those who did not use at all. Participants included 1300 people from a variety of backgrounds 200 of which were undergraduate students and 100 of the author's acquaintances who then forwarded the email to the other. The participants were given a survey about their marijuana use, an Apathy Evaluation Scale to measure motivation, and a Satisfaction with Life Scale to measure subject well-being. From this study, it was concluded that marijuana does not have an effect on motivation; however, it did have a significant effect on subject well-being. Daily users of marijuana were found to have lower well-being than those who abstain from marijuana use (Barnwell, Earleywine, & Wilcox, 2006).

In Texas, researchers performed a very extensive study on marijuana use and motivation in the adolescent population. The participants ranged in age from 14 to 18 and were placed in two very strict groups of either DSM-IV marijuana addicts or non-users. Throughout the study, drug tests were administered to make sure that the marijuana users were still using only marijuana and no other drugs and that the control group, the non-users, were not using any drugs including marijuana. A laboratory measure of motivation was given to the participants that allowed them to either choose a non-work or work option to earn rewards. Participants were also given two tests to measure social and cognitive function, the Youth Self-Report and the Shipley Institute of Living Scale, at the end of the study. Results of this experiment were different than those of previous ones. From this study, it was concluded that there was a high correlation with marijuana dependence and lower motivation as measured by choosing the non-work option to obtain less reward. Experimenters even controlled for conduct disorders and cognitive aptitude to make sure the results were as accurate as possible. This rather intense study drew the conclusion that marijuana does indeed have an effect on motivation, at least in the adolescent population (Lane, Cherek, Pietras, & Steinberg, 2005).

Looking at more than just the effect marijuana has on motivation, researchers assessed the attributes of 44 occasional marijuana users versus 45 heavy marijuana users in a college population. Occasional smokers were defined as those who smoked less than 10 times a month at any time in their life while heavy smokers were those that smoked daily for at least two years. Attributes being measured by a series of questionnaires and surveys included demographic information, drug use, the Rand Mental Health Inventory, motivation, and mental disease. One solid finding was that heavy smokers had higher history of other substance abuse including hallucinogens and cocaine. Initially it was found that they also performed worse on memory and motivation measures but later that was disputed by comparing demographic, mental health, and family background yielding the results that heavy marijuana users and occasional marijuana users do not differ in any of the areas being tested (Kouri, Pope, Yurgelun-Todd, & Gruber, 1995).

Present Study

With the recent legalization of marijuana and its incidence of use on the rise, there are many wondering what sort of implications this could have on the citizens of the United States. Multiple studies have shown that marijuana use has negative health and psychological consequences. Some studies suggest that heavy marijuana use leads to lower motivation. The purpose of this research is to more thoroughly assess the relationship between marijuana use and motivation. It is hypothesized that increased marijuana use will be accompanied by decreased motivation as measured by the Achievement Motivation Inventory and increased apathy as measured by the Apathy Evaulation Scale.

METHODS

Participants

College students from a large Midwestern university along with the general public were participants in this study. The study was designed on Qualtrics, which is an online testing site. In order to recruit college students the study was available on SONA – an online database of studies that students enrolled in psychology classes on campus are able to access. Students participating in the study were compensated by one credit of extra credit for their particular psychology class. In order to obtain enough participants from the general public, the study was posted on multiple craigslist sites including Boston, New York, Denver, Jacksonville, and Los Angeles and offer a chance for compensation. Two participants will be randomly selected to receive a 25 dollar Amazon gift card. The number of participants was 195 (150 defined as non-users, 23 defined as occasional users, 22 defined as heavy users). Participants were asked about their marijuana usage in the last year. Heavy users were characterized as those who use marijuana three or more times a week; Occasional users were those who use two or more times a month; and non-users will be those who have not used marijuana at all in the past year.

Measures

Participants answered questions regarding age, sex, level of education completed, ethnicity, income, and occupation. In order to measure motivation, two different questionnaires were provided to participants. The first of which was the Apathy Evaluation Scale (AES) that was developed by Marin (1996). Apathy, the lack of interest, enthusiasm, or excitement, is actually the opposite of motivation. A 4-point Likert scale is used one each of the 18 questions to measure apathy; (1) being "Not at All" and (4) being "A lot" regarding how much each statement applies to the individual. Responses are scaled from 1 to 4, and scales can vary from 18 to 72 (Marin, 1996).

The Achievement Motivation Inventory (AMI), a broadly used test to measure achievement motivation was the second questionnaire assessing motivation. From this test, many different aspects of motivation are measured. This inventory consists of 170 questions, 10 questions from each 17 characteristics that make up motivation. A 7-point Likert format from (1) "Does not apply at all" to (7) "Applies fully to me" was used to answer how much the questions apply to participants. The 17 characteristics to measure motivation are compensatory effort, competitiveness, confidence in success, dominance, eagerness to learn, engagement, fearlessness, flexibility, flow, goal setting, independence, internality, persistence, preference for difficult tasks, pride in productivity, self-control, and status orientation (Schuler, Thorton, Frintrup, & Mueller Hanson, 2004).

RESULTS

Demographic Information

There were 237 participants recruited in this study; however, 42 participants were thrown out due to the following reasons – did not sign consent form, did not finish the survey, or completed the survey in seconds. Participants ranged from age 18 to age 52 with 82.7% were 18 to 21 years of age. There were no significant demographic differences across the three group (all p's > .14) with the exception of Income (Chi-Square = 19.11, p < .01).

Regarding marijuana use, 116 participants or 59.2 percent had used the substance before and 80 participants or 40.8 percent had not ever used the substance in their life. When asked about marijuana use over the past year, 76.5 percent of participants used less than 1 time per month, 11.7 percent used more than 2 times per month, and 11.2 percent used 1 or more times per week.

AES and AMI Analyses

AES scores did not differ across the Non-Users (M = 58.56, SD = 5.46), Occasional Users (M = 58.12, SD = 9.07) or Heavy Users (M = 57.05, SD = 6.07), F = .494, p = .611). For the AMI, Table 1 lists ANOVA results. A Bonferroni correction was performed in order to avoid any false positive results. Only three AMI subtests revealed significance across groups (Confidence in Success, Internality, Pride in Productivity). For *Confidence in Success*, only the difference between non-users and heavy users was significant (*p* = .035). For *Internality*, only the difference between non-users and occasional was significant (*p* = .005) and between often users and occasional users was significant (*p* = .004). For P*ride in Productivity* only occasional and often users differed (*p* = .039).

Table 1. Mean and Standard Deviation performance (and F and p values) across the three groups

	Non Users M (SD)	Occasional Users M (SD)	Heavy Users M(SD)	F value	*p* Value
Compensatory effort	31.36 (8.95)	34.26 (8.68)	31.36 (9.27)	1.07	.346
Competitiveness	35.40 (7.43)	33.91 (6.41)	37.14 (8.52)	1.02	.364
Confidence in success	31.11 (8.67)	31.96 (9.46)	26.05 (8.10) [a]	3.55	.031*
Dominance	35.86 (8.23)	35.30 (8.08)	33.13 (7.81)	1.07	.345
Eagerness to learn	37.70 (7.87)	35.68 (6.86)	34.95 (9.28)	1.58	.209
Engagement	34.51 (8.70)	34.17 (7.71)	36.45 (8.43)	0.16	.851
Fearlessness	33.90 (9.52)	32.09 (9.20)	38.32 (11.55)	2.58	.078
Flexibility	31.87 (7.70)	32.39 (8.98)	30.50 (6.43)	0.38	.682
Flow	33.60 (8.52)	32.34 (7.57)	30.14 (,8.62)	1.71	.183
Goal setting	33.19 (8.01)	34.14 (8.81)	32.14 (7.23)	0.34	.710
Independence	33.14 (7.12)	34.00 (7.27)	21.50 (6.55)	0.75	.476
Internality	40.91 (8.69)	34.77 (7.76) [a]	43.05 (7.25) [b]	6.24	.002*
Persistence	36.89 (7.94)	35.65 (7.32)	37.77 (6.05)	0.44	.645
Preference for doing difficult tasks	34.44 (6.89)	33.13 (6.31)	34.18 (6.95)	0.37	.692
Pride in productivity	24.47 (10.14)	28.48 (12.32)	20.86 (7.70) [b]	3.16	.045*
Self-control	38.83 (8.56)	34.91 (6.64)	38.59 (7.04)	2.28	.105
Status orientation	27.41 (9.46)	29.50 (10.79)	24.10 (7.62)	1.81	.155
Total AMI	578.24 (9.35)	562.84 (24.55)	557.43 (23.35)	.458	.633

DISCUSSION

The purpose of this study was to discover whether or not marijuana use could be correlated with decreased motivation or the "amotivational syndrome." Two tests were used to measure motivation – the Apathy Evaluation Scale (AES) and the Achievement Motivation Inventory (AMI). No significant group differences emerged for the AES scores, suggesting that increased marijuana use did not increase apathy.

Unlike the AES, the AMI results yielded significant findings. Although the overall AMI scores did not differ across the three groups, Confidence in Success, Internality, and Pride in Productivity did differ. For Confidence in Success, non-users had significantly higher scores than heavy users. Confidence in success is defined as the following – Confidence in achieving success even when there are obstacles to overcome. According to the AMI manual, respondents with high scores in this area anticipate that they will be successful in their efforts (Schuler, et al., 2004). For Internality significant differences between non-users and occasional users were observed as well as between occasional and heavy users. However, this relationship is not necessarily what is expected, with occasional users having significantly lower internality scores than the non-user and heavy user groups. Internality is the belief that one's successes are not due to situational variable, rather they are due to internal causes. Finally, Pride in Productivity, which is a sense of accomplishment and enjoyment that comes from simply doing the best one can, showed that occasional users had significantly higher scores than heavy marijuana users (Schuler, et al., 2004).

What are the implications of the findings in this study? First of all, marijuana may not be as harmful and debilitating of a drug as described by some scientists and psychologists. The suggested "amotivational syndrome" affecting heavy users of marijuana may just be more of a bad stereotype than an accurate description of the population. Also, marijuana's schedule I drug status may need to be re-evaluated. Marijuana is on the same drug status as drugs such a heroin and cocaine, which could be looked at as an extreme, harsh categorization of the drug. Changing the drug status would result in fewer government restrictions on medical marijuana research. Allowing more research could lead to new medical discoveries, whether positive or negative, about the currently illicit drug. Also, the safest chemical contents could be determined by the Food and Drug Administration. It is important that more research is done on the motivational relationship.

There were also some limitations. First, anytime a self-report survey is used, participant self-report error may be taken into account. Participants worry that their responses may be judged even though they are told that the survey is anonymous. Participants may have unknowingly incorrectly rated themselves higher or lower on certain traits asked by the questionnaires. Surveys are very subjective and not the most accurate measure. Unfortunately, motivation is not an easily measured, clear-cut trait – similar to many psychological traits. Because the survey was rather lengthy, particularly the AMI that consisted of 170 questions, it may be possible that participants did not clearly read the questions and their responses were not as thought out as they could have been. Second, the design of this study could be improved. For some of the questions asked, participants were allowed to type their own responses. This made it difficult to uniformly code, and some participants' responses were not clear cut and easy to interpret due to errors in spelling or misunderstanding of the questions. For example, participants were asked to fill in their occupation. It was hard to determine whether or not the participants consider whether or not being a student was an occupation so there may be some self-report error in that area of demographic information. Also, some participants who were students may have answered their part-time or summer job, not their current occupation as a student. In a future study, including hours spent at one's occupation could be used as a means of measuring motivation to discover whether or not marijuana use affects work performance. Third, in regards to marijuana use the categories were defined as the following – non users using less than one time per month, occasional users using two or more times per month, and often users using one or more times per week. There is a gap between the non-user group and occasional user group not accounting for those who use 2 times per month. Also, occasional users had a minimum amount but not a maximum amount per month. Participants most likely categorized themselves at their own discretion, leading to inaccurate categories of use. Because this is the main variable in the study, this is a rather large issue and could have an effect on results. Fourth, we could have used actual tasks rather than paper and pencil measures of motivation. This would be an effective means of measuring motivation as it could take away the self-report bias that the AMI and AES have. In future studies, using the AMI and AES along with a task measure of motivation may provide more accurate, reliable results on how marijuana use is correlated with motivation. Fifth, in order to infer causation variables must be manipulated. For example, participants would have to all have never used marijuana before and complete the motivation assessment followed by completing the survey months or years later with the use of marijuana being manipulated. Ideally, a longitudinal study that followed those who did not use the drug initially and comparing their motivational measures before and after use with those who consistently did not use would be the most effective way at determining whether marijuana had a tru effect on its users' motivation.

In conclusion, marijuana is a mind altering substance and heavy use of the drug is correlated with lower motivation and higher apathy. With the legalization of the drug spreading across the United States like wild-fire, there is convincing evidence that negative consequences will come with marijuana legalization assuming that use will go up due to the drug's legal status. As for this particular study, increased marijuana use did not result in increased apathy and decreased motivation on the part of the heavy users. However we did see group differences is some aspects of Achievement Motivation. Future studies need to follow up on these group differences.

REFERENCES

Barwell, S., Earleywine, M. & Wilcox, R. (2006). Cannabis, motivation, and life satisfaction in an internet sample. *Subst Abuse Treat Prev Policy*, *1*, 2.

Boyette, C. & Wilson, J. (2015). It's 2015? Is weed legal in your state. *CNN.* Retrieved from: http://www.cnn.com/2015/01/07/us/recreational-marijuana-laws/.

Budney, A., Roffman, R., Stephens, R. & Walker, D. (2007). Marijuana dependence and its treatment. *Pubmed Central*, *1*, 4-16.

Duncan, D. (1987). Lifetime Prevalence of "Amotivational Syndrome" Among Users and Non-users of Hashish. *Psychology of Addictive Behavior*, *1*, 114-119.

Dupont, R. (1997). The Selfish Brain. American Psychiatric Press, Inc.

ElSohly, M. & Slade, D. (2005). Chemical constituents of marijuana: The complex mixture of natural cannabinoids. *Life Science*, *78*, 2005.

Fibley, F., Sina, Aslan, C., Vince, D., Spence, J., Damarius, E., Caprihan, A. & Segall, J. (2014). Long-term effects of marijuana on the brain. *Proceedings of the National Academic Society*, *111*, 16,913-16,918.

Goldstein, A. (2001). *Addiction: From biology to drug policy.*

Halikas, J. A., Weller, R. A., Morse, C. & Shapiro, T. (1982). Incidence and characteristics of amotivational syndrome, including findings, among chronic marijuana users. In Marijuana and youth: Clinical observations on motwation and learning (DHHS Publication No. ADM 82-1186). Washington, DC: U.S. Government Printing Office.

Iverson, L. (2003). Cannabis and the brain. *Brain*, *126*, 1252-1270.

Justinova, Z., Goldberg, S., Heishman S. & Tanda, G. (2005). Self-administration of cannabinoids by experimental animals and human marijuana smokers. *PMC*, *81 (2)*, 285-299.

Khoury, M., Gorgievski, V., Moutsimilli, L., Giross, B. & Tzavara, E. (2012). Interactions between cannabinoid and dopaminergic pathway: Evidence From animal studies. *Progress in Neuro-Psychopharmacology and Biological Psychiatry*, *38*, 36-50.

Kouri, E., Pope, Jr. H., Yurgelun-Todd, D. & Gruber, S. (1995). Attributes of heavy vs. occasional marijuana smokers in a college population. *Biology Psychiatry*, *37*, 475-481.

Lane, S., Cherek, D., Pietras, C. & Steinberg, J. (2005). Performance of heavy marijuana-smoking adolescents of a laboratory measure of motivation. *Addictive Behaviors*, *30*, 815-828.

Madras, B. (2014). Dopamine challenge reveals neuroadaptive changes in marijuana users. *Proceedings of the National Academy of Sciences of the United States of America, 111*, 11915–11916.

Marin, R. S. (1996). Apathy: Concept syndrome neural mechanisms and treatment. *Seminars Clin Neuropsychiatry*, *1*, 304-314.

Mikuriya, T. (1969). Marijuana in Medicine. *California Medicine*, 34-40.

Schuler, H., Thornton III, G., Frintrup, A. & Mueller-Hanson, R. (2004). *Achievement motivation inventory manual.* Cambridge, MA: Hoegrefe & Huber Publishers.

In: Marijuana
Editor: Margie Vasquez
ISBN: 978-1-63484-409-3

Chapter 2

MEDICAL MARIJUANA: MEDICAL NECESSITY VS. POLITICAL AGENDA

***Peter A. Clark*[1], *SJ, PhD, Kevin M. Capuzzi*[2], *JD, and Cameron Fick*[3]**

[1]Professor of Medical Ethics,
Director of the Institute of Clinical Bioethics,
Saint Joseph's University, Philadelphia, PA, US
[2]Pinckney, Harris and Weidinger, LLC,
Wilmington, Delaware, US
[3]Georgetown Medical School,
Georgetown University. Washington, DC, US

ABSTRACT

Marijuana is classified by the Drug Enforcement Agency (DEA) as an illegal Schedule I drug which has no accepted medical use. However, recent studies have shown that medical marijuana is effective in controlling chronic non-cancer pain, alleviating nausea and vomiting associated with chemotherapy, treating wasting syndrome associated with AIDS, and controlling muscle spasms due to multiple sclerosis. These studies state that the alleviating benefits of marijuana outweigh the negative effects of the drug, and recommend that marijuana be administered to patients who have failed to respond to other therapies.

Despite supporting evidence, the DEA refuses to reclassify marijuana as a Schedule II drug, which would allow physicians to prescribe marijuana to suffering patients. The use of medical marijuana has continued to gain support among states, and is currently legal in 23 states and the District of Columbia and Guam. This is in stark contrast to the federal government's stance of zero-tolerance, which has led to a heated legal debate in the United States. After reviewing relevant scientific data and grounding the issue ethically, there is a strong argument for allowing physicians to prescribe marijuana for medical purposes. Patients have a right to all beneficial treatments and to deny them this right violates their basic human rights.

Debate about medical marijuana is challenging the basic foundations of the accepted practice in the medical, legal and ethical communities. A major criticism of alternative therapies like medical marijuana is they have not been scientifically tested, leading many to question their safety and efficacy [1]. However, proponents in the medical community argue for medical marijuana use based on its effectiveness in managing debilitating pain, nausea and vomiting associated with chemotherapy, as well as its efficacy in treating severe weight loss commonly experienced by AIDS sufferers. Medical marijuana can be used as a stand-alone treatment for these conditions or as a complement to conventional ones in order to help patients better withstand the conventional treatments' effects and thereby obtain the full benefit, whether a cure or improvement of their condition [2]. In recognition and acceptance of the effectiveness of medical marijuana, twenty-three states and the District of Columbia and Guam have approved initiatives to make marijuana legal for medicinal purposes [3], including Alaska, Arizona, California, Colorado, Connecticut, Delaware, Hawaii, Illinois, Maine, Maryland, Michigan, Massachusetts, Minnesota, Montana, New Hampshire, Nevada, New Jersey, New Mexico, New York, Oregon, Rhode Island, Vermont, and Washington, as well as the District of Columbia and Guam. However, the leading opponent to legalization is the federal government, which has continued to trump state law rights by threatening patients and physicians with criminal prosecution and closing dispensaries users and prescribers rightfully believed such action to be legal.

The history of marijuana use for medicinal purposes extends back through millennia. The medical use of marijuana can be traced back to 2737 B.C., when Emperor Shen Neng was prescribing marijuana tea to treat gout, rheumatism, malaria, and even poor memory [4]. The drug's popularity spread throughout Asia to the Middle East and into Africa, and many ancient physicians prescribed marijuana for numerous ailments, from pain relief to childbirth [5]. In Western medicine, between 1840 and 1900, more than 100 articles citing marijuana's therapeutic qualities were published in American and European medical journals. These early American medical journals were recommending hemp seeds and roots for conditions including inflamed skin, incontinence and venereal disease, and in 1851, the United States Pharmacopoeia included hemp in its catalog of medicines. Marijuana was routinely prescribed by American physicians and enjoyed legal status in the United States until 1937 when U.S. legislature passed the first federal law against marijuana – the Marihuana Tax Act. This Act imposed a $1 per ounce tax on marijuana purchased for medical intention [6]. Later, in the 1950s, Congress passed the Boggs Act and the Narcotics Control Act, which outlined mandatory sentences for drug offenders, including marijuana possessors and distributors [4]. Eventually, the 1970 Uniform Controlled Substance Act classified marijuana as a Schedule I drug, thus making possession of a Schedule I drug like marijuana, heroin, ecstasy, LSD, GHB and peyote illegal [6]. Under this Act, there are five schedules of drugs – Schedule I, II, III, IV, and V. A Schedule I drug has a high potential for abuse, and has no accepted medical use in treatment due to a lack of accepted safety for use of the drug. A Schedule II drug has a high potential for abuse like a Schedule I drug, but it has an accepted medical use for treatment. Schedule III, IV, and V drugs have a low potential for abuse and are accepted for medical treatment. The federal government's basis for threatening prosecution is due to the 1970 classification of marijuana as a Schedule I drug [7].

While the subject of medical marijuana is becoming an increasingly heated medical issue, it also continues to stir the embers of legal arguments. Advocates on both sides continue to battle at federal and state government levels. One such state where legal battles have raged is Montana. Montana's state legislature legalized the medical use of marijuana in 2004 [8], but in the past year, Montana residents have seen increased legal opposition to this ruling. The issue of medical marijuana is now firmly encased in the halls of the judicial system in states like Montana and California. In California, there are now certain cities like Anaheim that have taken their case to ban marijuana dispensaries to the local courts. In August 2011, an Orange County Superior Court Judge ruled that the restriction of distribution of medical-marijuana in Anaheim was not a contradiction to state law. The judge supported his ruling by saying that state legislature allows local laws to "fill in the gaps that exist in state medical-marijuana law" [9].

As certain states seem to be backtracking, other states like Delaware, Pennsylvania, and nine others (Alabama, Connecticut, Idaho, Illinois, Massachusetts, New Hampshire, New York, North Carolina, Ohio) [10] are striving to create a future environment where medical marijuana is legal. Delaware, the most recent state to legalize medical marijuana, signed a bill into law on May 13, 2011 [11]. Pennsylvania has not yet voted on the issue, but in 2009, it proposed a bill for medical marijuana legalization [12].

The ethical dilemma at the core of this debate is whether the federal ban on the use of medical marijuana violates the physician-patient relationship. The argument can be framed by the ethical principles of autonomy and beneficence. Patients have the right to expect full disclosure and discussion of all available treatment options from their physicians. Denying a patient knowledge of and access to a therapy that relieves pain and suffering, especially when the patient has a terminal disease, violates the basic duty of a physician. As a result, physicians find themselves at the center of this controversy, searching for a compromise between medical necessity and government restrictions.

The main objection to the medical use of marijuana by the federal government is largely attributable today to a national policy of zero-tolerance toward illicit drugs. This objection is extended to include a prohibition on legalizing marijuana for medical purposes as well, and is underscored by three suppositions initially outlined during the Clinton Administration. First, marijuana is an illegal drug that remains unproven in terms of safety or efficacy. Second, it is argued that marijuana is a "gateway drug" that leads to more serious drug use. Third, any legalization of marijuana for medical purposes will send the wrong message to the public, and in particular to our children, namely that marijuana is acceptable for recreational use and even beneficial [13].

With regard to documenting the effectiveness of medical marijuana, the most comprehensive analysis to date in medical literature was issued on March 17, 1999, by a White House-commissioned committee of 11 independent scientists appointed by the Institute of Medicine. The researchers concluded that, "the benefits of smoking marijuana were limited by the toxic effects of the smoke, but nonetheless recommended that the drug be given under close supervision to patients who do not respond to other therapies" [14]. The report continues that, "there was no evidence that giving the drug to sick people would increase illicit drug use in the general population. Nor is marijuana a 'gateway drug' that prompts patients to use harder drugs like cocaine and heroin" [15]. This government-sponsored study presented solid scientific data that indicates the potential therapeutic value of marijuana in controlling some forms of pain, alleviating nausea and vomiting, treating wasting due to AIDS, and combating muscle spasms associated with multiple sclerosis (MS). Neither does it increase drug usage or lead to harder drugs [16]. Despite their own findings, the federal government continues to prohibit this effective drug from being prescribed by physicians for patients suffering from specific treatment side-effects, which have lead to strong objections to the government's stance by medical researchers, physicians, legal experts, and ethicists, not to mention the patients that rely on marijuana to improve their medical condition.

Attempts to reassign marijuana to a Schedule II drug classification have been rejected by the Drug Enforcement Administration (DEA). The basis for rejection is the assertion that, "there was no scientific evidence showing that marijuana was better than other approved drugs for any specific medical condition" [17]. The federal government's argument is further asserted to have logical grounding, to wit: marijuana is an illegal drug; no one should ever use illegal drugs; therefore, no one should ever use marijuana for any reason [13]. Other opponents of the legalization of medical marijuana, such as certain members of the medical community and anti-marijuana organizations, assert that marijuana is too dangerous for medical use, it lacks FDA approval, and that several legal drugs make marijuana use unnecessary [18]. Today, the DEA maintains this position outlined under the Clinton Administration and, in July 2011, ruled that marijuana has "no accepted medical use" and should therefore remain illegal under federal law, in spite of differing state legislation allowing medical marijuana [19]. However, with scientific evidence pointing to the contrary, some perceive the government's treatment of this issue as more of a political matter than a medical issue.

The purpose of this article, therefore, is fourfold: first, to explore the medical aspect of marijuana by examining pertinent scientific research; second, to study the legal issues related to medical marijuana legalization; third, to provide an ethical analysis of the arguments for and against medical marijuana legalization; and fourth, to conclude with specific recommendations.

Medical Perspective

Marijuana is taken from the leaves and flowering tops of the hemp plant, *Cannabis sativa*, which grows in most regions of the world. *C. sativa* contains over 460 known compounds, of which 60 are cannabinoids, or compounds unique to cannabis. The main psychoactive compound of marijuana is delta-9-tetrahydrocannabinol (THC) [20].

The harmful effects of marijuana include rapid heartbeat, some loss of coordination, and impaired immediate memory. In addition, the drug can adversely affect one's critical skills, including those skills necessary to operate vehicles safely, such as judgment of distance and reaction time [21]. As reported by a 2010 Harvard Medical Study, marijuana seems to induce psychotic symptoms and worsen conditions in patients already diagnosed with schizophrenia or other psychotic disorders. One such study of more than 50,000 young Swedish soldiers found that those who had smoked marijuana at least once were more than twice as likely to develop schizophrenia as those nonsmokers. For those who said they had used marijuana more than 50 times, research showed that they were six times more likely to develop schizophrenia as the nonsmokers. More evidence is being gathered demonstrating early or heavy marijuana use might not only trigger psychosis in people who are already susceptible, but might also cause psychosis in some people who might not otherwise have developed it; however, direct cause and effect cannot be asserted with absolute certainty from that individual study [22].

Further risks associated with marijuana found in the 2010 study include addiction, anxiety and mood disorders. Observational studies suggest that every one out of nine people who regularly smoke marijuana become dependent on it, especially when smoked for an extended amount of time. One such contributing factor may be the THC concentration in the herbal form of marijuana. In the United States, as well as Europe, THC concentration in marijuana sold used to range from 1% to 4%, but it appears that this number has risen to 7%. Even though many marijuana users state that marijuana calms them down, for others, this is not the case. The most commonly reported side effects of smoking marijuana are intense anxiety and panic attacks. Studies show that 20% to 30% of marijuana users experience said side effects, and that a higher dose of THC has also proven to increase anxiety episodes. Marijuana may also induce manic episodes and increase rapid cycling between manic and depressive moods in patients with bipolar disorder, but it is not fully understood if marijuana users are at an increased risk of developing bipolar disorder. Several observational studies have also revealed that, for some users, marijuana may increase symptoms of depression and increase the risk of developing depression. Also, the government's assertion that marijuana is a gateway drug that may lead to harder drugs has not been proven and is less conclusive than any of the above mentioned medical risks [22].

There are also a number of other medical risks associated with marijuana. First, it is difficult to determine the effective dosage of smoked marijuana, since the concentration of the active ingredient, THC, varies according to the particular plant and how it is grown. Second, nonconclusive studies have shown that THC both suppresses macrophages and human T-lymphocytes and enhances macrophage secretion of interleukin-I [23]. These are critical components of the immune system and could seriously jeopardize AIDS patients who use marijuana. Other studies emphasize the potential for toxic compounds in marijuana smoke, which include harmful cannabinoids, gases, and other particulates. Studies have shown that marijuana tar contains 50% more phenols than tobacco tar [24]. Finally, marijuana can also be contaminated by microorganisms and fungi, which can cause possible infections by pathogenic organisms. There have been reported cases of marijuana smokers contracting pulmonary fungal infections. In addition, adulterants such as pesticides and fertilizers can compromise the purity of the marijuana [25]. To combat these risks, various methods, such as filtering marijuana in water pipes and vaporizing the marijuana, have been shown to remove certain toxins and to deliver a higher cannabinoid-to-tar ratio than do cigarettes or pipes. Also, sterilizing the marijuana by dry heat (300°F) kills spores and fungi [26]. These risks can be minimized further if the supply of marijuana is grown under government-regulated conditions rather than illicit sources.

Although there are some medical concerns, from a clinical standpoint, in controlled situations such as ones being recommended by proponents of medical use, the positive effects would seem to greatly outweigh the negative ones. Several clinical findings have documented marijuana's efficacy in treating pain, neurological and movement disorders, nausea of patients undergoing chemotherapy for cancer, loss of appetite and weight (cachexia) related to AIDS, and glaucoma [27]. Despite clinical findings in support of medical marijuana, the DEA has classified marijuana as an illegal Schedule I drug which has "no accepted medical use." The DEA will not reschedule marijuana without an official determination of the safety and efficacy from the Food and Drug Administration (FDA).

In order to reschedule marijuana, the FDA requires controlled, double-blind clinical trials for this to occur. However, there is a major obstacle preventing these trials. Like all other herbal medicines, marijuana faces a major roadblock that inhibits conducting sophisticated clinical trials: a lack of patentable product [28]. Without the financial incentive of being able to patent the substance as a commercial product, few have pursued the path of carrying out research using the sophisticated, difficult, and expensive procedures proscribed by best practice.

Another federal restriction is the requirement that clinical studies be funded from scarce grant money controlled by the National Institutes of Health (NIH) [28]. These restrictions have discouraged researchers from studying the medical benefits of marijuana. For example, the 2012 estimate for clinical research on cancer accounts for approximately six billion dollars of the NIH budget, which totals 31.2 billion dollars [29]. The 2011 NIH budget allocated the following funds available for marijuana research for qualified organizations: $2 million in 4-5 awards. According to NIH Grant guidelines on marijuana, applicants may request budgets with direct costs up to $500,000 per year for a maximum period of 5 years. Therefore, the total budget would be $10 million over the 5 year period [30]. Of the yearly NIH budget of approximately $31.2 billion, the $2 million going toward marijuana research can be calculated as comprising 0.006% of the yearly budget, thus illustrating how marijuana research is vastly underfunded.

Controlled clinical studies would need to manage medical testing of marijuana and its various forms. Today, smoked marijuana is not the only form in circulation. There are a number of forms of marijuana that are used for medical purposes, including a synthetic form, Marinol (dronabinol), which is taken orally [31]. Marinol, manufactured by Unimed Pharmaceuticals, Inc., is a Schedule III prescription drug [19], approved by the FDA in 1985 for treatment of nausea and vomiting of cancer chemotherapy patients who have not responded to the conventional antiemetic therapy. In 1992, the FDA also approved it for use in loss of appetite and weight loss related to AIDS. However, there are three major concerns associated with Marinol [32]. First, some patients complained that the effects of the pill were too strong at first, and then wore off quickly [33]. Second, it is very expensive, costing patients anywhere from $200-$800 monthly [34]. Third, Marinol can be difficult for nauseous patients to consume; some patients fail to keep the pill down long enough for it to be effective [35].

Another synthetic marijuana-based drug is Nabilone, a Schedule II drug, similar to Marinol, used to treat nausea and vomiting. Nabilone uses a moderately different preparation of synthetic THC, which makes it more completely absorbed into the bloodstream as compared to Marinol [22]. Nabilone is now a controlled drug; however, *Nabilone* is perceived to produce more undesirable side effects, have a longer onset of action and to be more expensive than smoked cannabis [36]. The cost associated with Nabilone is $20 for a 1-mg capsule, and the estimated cost per year is $4000 [37].

Another form used in Canada is a spray alternative called Sativex [38]. In 2006, the Food and Drug Administration (FDA) issued an investigational new drug (IND) application for Sativex. The IND allows a drug to be studied with the goal of approving it for marketing if it is deemed safe and effective [19]. More recently, in 2010, the efficacy of Sativex for bladder dysfunction as a symptom of multiple sclerosis (MS) was tested. It was a 10 week, double-blind, randomized, placebo-controlled, parallel-group trial in 135 subjects with MS and overactive bladder. Researchers concluded that Sativex did have an impact on MS patients with overactive bladder, citing some improvement in symptoms associated with the patients' bladder dysfunction [39]. Sativex is now a controlled drug, and has recently been licensed for managing MS [40]. One of the biggest problems with Sativex is the cost. A vial of Sativex that lasts 10 days costs $124.95 in Canada, which amounts to about $375 monthly [38]. More recently legalized in Britain, a 10 milliliter vial (enough for 11 days) costs £125 [41], or approximately 205 U.S. dollars.

In relation to smoked marijuana, all of these alternatives are just that – alternatives, and not necessarily as effective. It has been argued that smoked marijuana is substantially more effective than these alternatives. The THC in the inhaled smoke is absorbed within seconds and is delivered to the brain rapidly and efficiently, as would be expected of a highly lipid-soluble drug. Maximum blood concentrations are reached about the time smoking is finished and then rapidly dissipate. Psychopharmacologic effects peak at 30 to 60 minutes. The clear advantage of smoked marijuana is the rapid onset and dissipation of effects, because the patient is able to self-titrate the dose. In addition, the plant contains many other compounds (including about 60 cannabinoids) that may produce some additional benefits [42].

Looking to the future, there may be safer alternatives on the horizon, including a medical marijuana patch. Medical Marijuana Delivery Systems (MMDS) LLC announced in February that it had obtained U.S. patent rights to a medical marijuana patch. MMDS will market the patch under the name Tetracan, and are hopeful that the patch will be available at dispensaries in approved states across the US by the end of 2011. The company continues to work on other delivery systems like creams, gels and oils [43]. Another alternative to smoking marijuana is ingesting the drug directly. Baking marijuana directly into foods is another way to reap the benefits of marijuana while avoiding the toxic effects of smoking the drug.

Oncologists were among the first medical professionals to advocate for the medical use of smoked marijuana. Reacting to a DEA suggestion that only a "fringe group" of oncologists accepted marijuana as an antiemetic agent, a random survey of the members of the American Society of Oncology was conducted in 1990. More than 1000 oncologists responded to the survey; 44% reported that they had recommended marijuana to at least one patient. Smoked marijuana was believed to be more effective than oral Marinol by the respondents. Of those who believed they had sufficient information to compare the two drugs directly, 44% believed smoked marijuana was more effective and 13% that Marinol was more effective [44]. In addition, the cost of smoked marijuana is considerably cheaper. "The cost of producing cannabis is about a dollar an ounce, and medical distribution would add at most a few more dollars. There are about 60 marijuana cigarettes in an ounce, and the average dose is one cigarette or less" [45].

A 2003 survey of 400 physicians, both general practitioners and specialists in the Netherlands, was performed just before the legal introduction of medicinal cannabis. Only 6% said that, under no condition, were they willing to prescribe medicinal marijuana, while 60% to 70% regarded medicinal cannabis sufficiently socially accepted and would prescribe it if asked for by a patient [46].

Scientific research on the medical effects of marijuana has been limited due to the stipulation that all studies must be funded by the National Institutes of Health. However, since 1978, the federal government has provided 20 patients with medical marijuana under a compassionate investigation new drug program. The Institute of Drug Abuse pays the University of Mississippi to grow a consistent, reliable source of research-grade cannabis. This is a pure (unadulterated and standardized) form of marijuana without contaminants or pesticides. A North Carolina manufacturer receives $62,000 a year from the federal government to roll the marijuana cigarettes and ship them in sealed tins of 300 cigarettes, to the patients' doctors and pharmacists. Each participant was given a letter from the FDA authorizing them to use this illegal substance that can bring a federal prison term of five years. In 1991, the federal government terminated this program, which was the only legal way to obtain access to marijuana. This program was terminated because, in the government's opinion, too many people became aware of the program and were asking for access to medical marijuana supplies. Twelve individuals were receiving marijuana cigarettes in 1991 and they were "grandfathered" when the program was terminated. Since that time, four individuals have died from AIDS and the remaining eight continue to receive their supply of marijuana cigarettes [47]. While the federal government at one time appeared to be moving toward acceptance and perhaps legalization of medical marijuana, it has instead decided to allow this program to disappear through attrition.

In February 1997, the National Institutes of Health released its report on the results of an expert panel that was convened to investigate the therapeutic potential of marijuana and to identify future research avenues that would be most productive. The panel of experts identified five areas where there was at least a suggestion of therapeutic value of marijuana and for which further study was indicated. The five areas were: (1) stimulates appetite and alleviates cachexia (severe weight loss), (2) controls nausea and vomiting associated with cancer chemotherapy, (3) decreases intraocular pressure for those suffering from glaucoma, (4) analgesia (pain reliever), and (5) neurologic and movement disorders are relieved. The group also concluded that more extensive studies were needed to fully evaluate the potential of marijuana as supportive care for cancer patients. Suggested areas of study were a smoke-free delivery system of marijuana's active ingredient THC, effects of marijuana on the lungs and immune system, and the dangerous byproducts of smoke marijuana [48].

On March 17, 1999, a panel of 11 independent experts at the Institute of Medicine released an extensive analysis of the medical uses of marijuana. This two-year study was ordered and financed by the White House Office of National Drug Control Policy. The report cautioned that the benefits of smoking marijuana were limited because the smoke in itself is so toxic. Yet at the same time, the panel of experts recommended that marijuana be given, on a short-term basis under close supervision, to patients who did not respond to other therapies. The panel believed that because of the toxicity of the smoke, the true benefits of marijuana would only be realized when alternative methods like capsules, patches and bronchial inhalers were developed to deliver more active components, called cannabinoids, without the harmful carcinogens of the smoke. The researchers recommended that the government should take the lead in developing more effective cannabinoid drugs. However, realizing this would take years to develop, the panel recommended that people, who do not respond to other therapy, be permitted to smoke marijuana in the interim. In addition to these recommendations, the report also contained new findings about the effects of marijuana on various medical conditions. In addition to the usefulness of medical marijuana in treating pain, nausea, and weight loss associated with AIDS, the report concluded that despite popular belief, marijuana was not useful in treating glaucoma. Marijuana does reduce some eye pressure associated with glaucoma; however, the effects were short-term, and did not outweigh the long-term hazards of using the drug. In addition, the study found there was little evidence that marijuana had any effect on movement disorders such as Parkinson's disease or Huntington's disease, but it was effective in combating the muscle spasms associated with MS [49].

Following the release of the Institute of Medicine's report on medical marijuana in 1999, evidence supporting medical marijuana has increased. In the last three years, cannabinoids have been found to help kill breast cancer cells [50], fight liver cancer [51], reduce inflammation [52], have antipsychotic effects [53] and even potentially help stave off the development of Alzheimer's disease [54] and reduce progression of Huntington's disease [55].

Most recently in 2011, cannabinoids' treatment of chronic non-cancer pain was examined using a randomized controlled trial. The cannabinoids studied were smoked cannabis, oromucosal extracts of cannabis based medicine, nabilone, Marinol and a novel THC analog. The non-cancer pain conditions were neuropathic pain, fibromyalgia, rheumatoid arthritis, and mixed chronic pain. Of the eighteen trials, fifteen showed a significant analgesic effect of cannabinoid compared to the placebo, and more importantly, there were no serious adverse effects. The overall results of the study stated that cannabinoids are safe and modestly effective in the treatment of the above mentioned non-cancer pain [56].

In October of 2009, the Office of the Deputy U.S. Attorney General issued a memorandum titled, "Investigation and Prosecutions in States Authorizing the Medical Use of Marijuana." The memorandum stated that the federal government would abstain from prosecuting individuals who are in compliance with state laws that allowed for the medical use of marijuana, but clearly stated that the government did not "legalize marijuana or provide a legal defense to a violation of federal law" [57].

However, once again, the government seems to be contradicting itself. While states increased regulation to protect and improve the structure of the medical marijuana industry in their states, despite guidelines set forth in the memorandum, federal prosecutors continued to assert themselves in these states, with acts like raids and strongly worded letters to governors. As of May 2011, letters have been sent to governors in Arizona, Colorado, Montana, Rhode Island, Vermont and Washington, which has made some states like Rhode Island, Montana and Washington revise or shift away from their plans to make a more mainstream medical marijuana industry. In Washington, Governor Christine Gregoire responded to a letter she received on the matter by asking for clarification from Washington's two United States attorneys. They responded to the governor's request by stating that the government would prosecute "vigorously against individuals and organizations that participate in unlawful manufacturing and distribution activity involving marijuana, even if such activities are permitted under state law" [58]. Supporters of medical marijuana believe that the federal government is sending mixed signals, but as a spokeswoman for the Justice Department said, "This is not a change in policy. It's a reiteration of the guidance that was handed down in 2009 by the deputy attorney general" [58].

The original state to legalize medical marijuana, California, has seen its share of crackdowns in the past few years. As federal enforcement was relaxed in 2009, the number of dispensaries skyrocketed. Cities like San Diego, San Francisco, and Los Angeles have now begun to raid and close several dispensaries. In Los Angeles, for example, one series of raids closed approximately 40 dispensaries [59].

As stated earlier, the DEA ruled in July 2011 that marijuana has "no accepted medical use" and should therefore remain illegal under federal law [12]. This ruling came in response to a 2002 petition filed by medical marijuana advocates asking for a reclassification of marijuana as a Schedule III, IV, or V drug. This may seem like a setback to advocates, however, it may in fact be an advance. The petition was filed in 2002, and after much delay, the government has finally ruled, which now allows advocates to appeal the government's ruling in federal court. This is not the first time a petition to reclassify marijuana has been rejected. Twice before has such a petition been rejected – the first in 1972 (denied 17 years later) and the second in 1995 (denied six years later) [60]. Both decisions were appealed by advocates, but the courts upheld the rejections and sided with the federal government.

As a result of this medical research, 16 states, as well as the District of Columbia, have approved ballot initiatives making marijuana legal for medical purposes [3]. One of the first states to do so was Arizona. In the November 1996 elections, Arizona voters passed Proposition 200 by a vote of 65% to 35%. Arizona law mandated that the prescribing physician must: document that scientific research exists which supports the use of a Schedule I substance for this purpose, receive written consent from the patient, and obtain the written opinion of a second medical doctor that the prescription is appropriate. The major concern of the Arizona proposition was that it allowed physicians to prescribe any Schedule I drug. To rectify this, the Arizona legislature amended the law to apply to only FDA-approved drugs in April 1997 [61]. A more recent state to approve medical marijuana was New Jersey in 2010. This legislation easily passed in both houses: 48-14 in the General Assembly and 25-13 in the State Senate [62]. New Jersey is one of the few states on the East Coast to approve legislation for medical marijuana, and has implemented more restrictive measures than original states like Arizona and California. According to New Jersey law, doctors are only allowed to prescribe marijuana for a set list of serious illnesses. Patients are forbidden from growing marijuana and using it in public, and are limited to two ounces of marijuana per month. These restrictive laws have attempted to eliminate the loopholes seen in other states where marijuana crackdowns have occurred. However, ever since the implementation of the guidelines set forth by states like Arizona and California, there has been a movement toward increasingly strict laws. As more states continue to legalize the medicinal use of marijuana, it would appear that the issue has become less about the medical issues, and more about the political implications.

Legal Perspective

While a strong case may be made for the medical and ethical bases in support of the legalization of medical marijuana, the United States' strong anti-drug stance [63] makes it impossible to view the issue without considering its legal effects. The legalization of medical marijuana invokes various fields of law. First and perhaps most obviously, is criminal law. As a Schedule I drug [64], the most serious classification under the current federal regime, marijuana is heavily regulated at the federal, state, and local levels. Second, issues of administrative law are raised by the rights of states to engage in rulemaking and pass legislation that is adverse to well-established federal criminal law precedent. Finally, health law is implicated. While overshadowed by the criminal and administrative law effects, medical marijuana raises important issues concerning doctors' and patients' rights, specifically medical autonomy, as well as medical malpractice issues such as overuse by patients, over-prescription by doctors for monetary gain, and use by non-patients, including second-hand consumption.

At its core, the legalization of medical marijuana presents a centuries-old struggle between federal and state rights. As explored in considerable detail herein, since the founding of this Nation, states have sought to govern their residents in a manner appropriate to the circumstances of that particular state and without interference from the federal government. For example, recollecting the discontent that ultimately gave rise to the Civil War, the southern states felt that the federal government was out of touch with their mainly agriculturally-based society compared to the northern states' mainly industrially-based society, and therefore believed that they ought to be able to govern themselves.

Even today, the distinction exists. Take for instance, Delaware and its pro-corporate laws which attract countless Fortune 500 companies to incorporate there [65]. While all but a few of the companies are headquartered in other states, they come to Delaware for its generous tax structure and well-established corporate case law. If Congress were to federalize corporate law, Delaware would certainly argue that the government was infringing on its rights as a state. Similarly, more than a dozen states have to some extent passed legislation legalizing medical marijuana, arguing in part that the individual medical needs of their residents is separate and distinct right from the federal government's right to regulate the use of marijuana.

To date, sixteen states and the District of Columbia have passed legislation legalizing medical marijuana; however, marijuana is a Schedule I drug under the Controlled Substances Act (CSA), 21 U.S.C. § 801, *et seq.* Congress, in enacting the CSA, recognized that although many controlled substances have a beneficial medical purpose, such purpose does not outweigh the important societal concern of conquering drug abuse and the legitimate and illegitimate trafficking of controlled substances. In particular, Congress made the following finding: "Many of the drugs included within [the CSA] have a useful and legitimate medicinal purpose and are necessary to maintain the health and general welfare of the American people." 21 U.S.C. § 801(1). So how are states permitted to enact legislation that so clearly runs afoul of established federal law? The answer to that question is complex and developed herein.

The United States Supreme Court, the final arbiter of legal matters in the Nation, has taken on the issue of medical marijuana only once. In 2005, the case of *Gonzalez v. Raich* (referred to herein as "*Raich*") dealt directly with whether the federal government could criminalize the use of medical marijuana that was legal under California's medical marijuana laws [66]. In 1996, California voters passed Proposition 215, now codified as the Compassionate Use Act of 1996 [67], to "create an exemption from criminal prosecution for physicians, as well as for patients and primary caregivers who possess or cultivate marijuana for medicinal purposes with the recommendation of approval of a physician" [68].

Angel Raich and another woman named Diane Monson were California residents who were prescribed marijuana by their licensed, board-certified family practitioners to alleviate pain associated with a myriad of medical conditions. Monson grew her own marijuana, while Raich relied on caregivers to provide hers. In 2002, county sheriffs and federal agents from the Drug Enforcement Agency came to Monson's home. After a three-hour standoff, county officials determined that Monson's marijuana use and cultivation was entirely lawful. Nonetheless, federal agents seized and destroyed all six of her marijuana plants as a violation of the CSA.

Monson joined with Raich to bring an action against the Attorney General of the United States [69] prohibiting the enforcement of the CSA for personal medicinal use provided by state law. At the District Court level [70], the District Court denied their motion for an injunction (a legal action effectively halting, in this case, government conduct). Raich and Monson appealed to the Federal Court of Appeals for the Ninth Circuit [71]. The Ninth Circuit reversed the District Court's ruling, holding that the use of medical marijuana pursuant to the Compassionate Use Act is a "separate and distinct" activity and sufficiently "different in kind from drug trafficking" prohibited by the CSA. The Department of Justice, on behalf of the Attorney General, then appealed the Ninth Circuit's decision to the Supreme Court.

The Supreme Court, in a divided 6-3 decision, reversed the Ninth Circuit and held that the federal government is acting squarely within its rights to criminalize the manufacture and possession of marijuana even where states approve its use for medicinal purposes. In support of its position, the Supreme Court cited an enumerate power of the Constitution, adopted in 1787, which provides that the federal government may "regulate Commerce with foreign Nations, and among the several States, and with the Indian Tribes" [72]. That power is known as the Commerce Clause.

Raich and Monson argued that the Commerce Clause was intended to apply only to the regulation of *interstate* commerce, not *intrastate* commerce, especially when done in the privacy of one's own home. The Supreme Court, citing a 1942 opinion [73], held that the federal government may regulate any activity that has a *substantial effect* on interstate commerce. The Supreme Court acknowledged that the federal government had to satisfy only the most-minimal burden of proof to determine that an activity has a substantial effect on interstate commerce. In the case of medical marijuana, the Supreme Court held that difficulties in distinguishing locally-cultivated and marijuana grown elsewhere, coupled with concerns of diversion into illicit channels, that the federal government met its burden for believing that the failure to regulate the *intrastate* manufacture and possession of marijuana would frustrate the Congressional intent of the CSA. Finally, the Supreme Court made clear that the fact that Raich and Monson used marijuana medicinally made no difference. Citing to what is known as the Constitution's Supremacy Clause

[74], the Supreme Court unambiguously stated that when there is a conflict between federal and state law, federal law prevails.

The Supreme Court's ruling in *Raich* would seem to effectively abolish all state laws legalizing the use of medical marijuana. Nonetheless, states continue to pass such laws. Thus, the tension between state and federal rights is ever-apparent. What many people do not realize, and it is unclear to what extent even prescribing physicians are aware, while a state law may legalize medical marijuana within a particular state, federal regulations – including criminal and civil penalties – still apply. Moreover, prescribing physicians must be cognizant of patients who reside, or even frequently travel to, a state other than that in which the physician practices or is licensed.

Further complicating this legal quagmire of state versus federal rights concerning the legalization of medical marijuana is that in October 2009, Attorney General Eric Holder issued a memorandum that the Department of Justice would stop enforcing the federal marijuana ban under the CSA against people who act in compliance with state medical marijuana laws. While this may at first appear as a victory for state rights, it should be carefully noted that a government memorandum has absolutely no legal precedence and would certainly not trump the Supreme Court's holding in *Raich*. The practical effect of the memorandum is only to delay the unresolved tension between state and federal rights in this area, as absent enforcement, the Supreme Court will not have another attempt to further develop its holding in *Raich*. In other words, it is just another hurdle in clearing the way to a decisive legal position in the matter.

Finally, the dispute between state and federal governments is not the only obstacle to a clear understanding of the legal status of medical marijuana. As discussed in the previous section, some local governments (cities, counties, etc.) in states that have legalized medical marijuana, now seek to impose their own regulations. Such is the case in the City of Anaheim, California, where on August 15, 2011 the Superior Court ruled in the case *Qualified Patients Association (QPA) v. City of Anaheim* that the City has the legal right to ban all medical marijuana dispensaries within the boundaries of the City. In short, the Court upheld a City Ordinance (Ordinance No. 6067), banning medical marijuana dispensaries as a public nuisance. The Court's decision, however, does not affect the use of medical marijuana or distribution through other legal means.

The Court in *QPA v. Anaheim* noted that Art. IX, § 7 of the California Constitution provides that "[a] county or city may make and enforce within its limits all local, police, sanitary, and other ordinances and regulations not in conflict with general laws" of California. One such permitted ordinance is that which abates a public nuisance." California law defines a public nuisance as "one which affects at the same time an entire community or neighborhood, or a considerable number of persons, although the extent of the annoyance or damage inflicted upon individuals may be unequal." The Court reasoned that mass distribution of medical marijuana through dispensaries, which are become largely unregulated, constitutes a public nuisance.

It is important to note that this is a decision at the trial court level which has no precedential value on anyone except the parties involved. It is likely that the proponents of the dispensaries will appeal to the appellate court and, if necessary, supreme court, where is a decision would have a more widespread effect. Nonetheless, the decision is significant as indicative of another avenue in which governments can use legal measures to defeat what was otherwise thought to be a "legal" state action.

From a health law perspective, physicians must carefully balance their medical and ethical responsibilities to their patients, with their own moral and legal responsibilities in following the law of the land. Although plausible after *Raich*, it is currently unclear to what extent a prescribing physician could be criminally charged with drug trafficking under the CSA or to what extent medical malpractice is implicated if a physician prescribes medical marijuana to a patient without explaining the possible legal consequences. Further, while that may not be the prescribing physician's legal duty to convey such information, it may be his or her medical or ethical duty in obtaining a patient's informed consent. If this analysis has shown anything, it is the paramount importance that prescribing physicians and patients alike are aware that the legal status of medical marijuana, despite of laws sixteen states and the District of Columbia, is entirely unresolved.

Ethical Perspective

Society, in general, has always recognized that in our complex world there is the possibility that we may be faced with a situation that has two consequences--one good and the other evil. The time-honored ethical principle that has been applied to these situations is called the principle of double effect. As the name itself implies, the human action has two distinct effects. One effect is the intended good; the other is unintended evil. As an ethical principle, it was never intended to be an inflexible rule or a mathematical formula, but rather it is to be used as an efficient guide to prudent moral judgment in solving difficult moral dilemmas [75]. The principle of double effect specifies four conditions which must be fulfilled for an action with both a good and an evil effect to be ethically justified:

1. The action, considered by itself and independently of its effects, must not be morally evil. The object of the action must be good or indifferent.
2. The evil effect must not be the means of producing the good effect.
3. The evil effect is sincerely not intended, but merely tolerated.
4. There must be a proportionate reason for performing the action, in spite of the evil consequences [76].

The principle of double effect is applicable to the issue of whether it is ethical for a physician to prescribe marijuana for medical reasons because it has two effects, one good and the other evil. The good effect is that smoked marijuana is more effective than conventional therapies in helping patients withstand the effects of accepted, traditional treatments which can bring about a cure or the amelioration of their condition. The evil effect is that marijuana smoke has toxic effects and as a Schedule I illegal drug it has been argued it could lead to more serious drug abuse and send a wrong message that illegal drug use is safe and even condoned. To determine if it is ethical for physicians to prescribe medical marijuana for patients as a medical therapy, this issue will be examined in light of the four conditions of the principle of double effect.

The first condition allows for the medical use of marijuana because the object of the action, in and of itself, is good. The moral object is the precise good that is freely willed in this action. The moral good of this action is to help treat pain, nausea, severe weight loss associated with AIDS and to combat muscle spasms associated with multiple sclerosis that cannot be treated adequately by traditional medicines. The immediate goal is not to endorse, encourage or promote illegal drug use. Rather, the direct goal is to relieve patients of their unnecessary pain and suffering [77]. The second condition permits the medical use of marijuana because the good effect of relieving pain and suffering is not produced by means of the evil effect. The two effects happen simultaneously and independently. The third condition is met because the direct intention of medical marijuana is to give patients suffering from life-threatening illnesses relief from the effects of accepted treatments that could cure their medical condition. Recent studies have shown that medical marijuana is more effective in controlling pain and nausea from chemotherapy treatments and in boosting the appetites of AIDS patient so as to combat wasting than any of the traditional FDA approved medications. To deny a physician the right to discuss, recommend, and prescribe marijuana to patients is a direct violation of the physician-patient relationship. To make an informed decision about their treatment, patients have the right to expect full disclosure and discussion of all available treatment options from their physicians. Failure to do this violates the patient's right of informed consent [78].

The hypothesized foreseen but unintended consequences of legalizing medical marijuana are two-fold. First, the smoke from marijuana is highly toxic and can cause lung damage. The intention of smoked marijuana is not to cause more health problems but to remedy the effects of existing treatments. Second, some members of the federal government believe that legalizing medical marijuana may lead to harder drug usage and may be seen as condoning and encouraging recreational drug use. Nevertheless, this has not been proven to be true. The March 17, 1999 report by the Institute of Medicine found no evidence that the medical use of marijuana would increase illicit use in the general population, nor was it a "gateway drug" that would lead to the use of harder drugs like cocaine or heroin [49]. According to bioethicist William Stempsey, M.D., the government's belief that "the availability of drugs on the street is a function of the availability of prescription drugs is wrong. Morphine and other narcotics are available at present only by prescription, and there is no widespread abuse of these drugs" [79]. In addition, a 1994 survey in *The New York Times* found that 17% of current marijuana users said they had tried cocaine, and only 0.2% of those who had not used marijuana had tried cocaine. Ethicist George Annas points out that there are two ways to interpret this study. One way is to conclude that those who smoke marijuana are 85 times as likely as others to try cocaine; another way is that 83% of pot smokers, or five out of six, never try cocaine [80]. A 2003 study by Jan van Ours of Tilburg University in the Netherlands, cannabis users typically start using the drug between the ages of 18 and 20, while cocaine use usually starts between 20 and 25. But it concludes that cannabis is not a stepping stone to using cocaine or heroin. Four surveys, covering nearly 17,000 people, were carried out in Amsterdam in 1987, 1990, 1994 and 1997. The study found that there was little difference in the probability of an individual taking up cocaine as to whether or not he or she had used cannabis. Although significant numbers of people in the survey did use soft and hard drugs, this was linked with personal characteristics and a predilection to experimentation [81]. If officials in the federal government are worried that the legalization of medical marijuana will send the wrong message to our children about drugs, then *Boston Globe* columnist Ellen Goodman asks a good question: "What is the infamous signal being sent to [children] ... if you hurry up and get cancer, you, too, can get high?" [82] Will some people view the legalization of medical marijuana as the condoning and encouraging of marijuana for recreational drug use? The answer is "yes." But this is not the direct intention of legalizing medical marijuana. The direct intention is to relieve pain and suffering that cannot be relieved by presently approved medications. This misinterpretation of the legalization of medical marijuana can be corrected through public education. Finally, the argument for the ethical justification of marijuana for medical use by the principle of double effect focuses on whether there is a proportionately grave reason for allowing the foreseen but unintended possible consequences. Proportionate reason is the linchpin that holds this complex moral principle together.

Proportionate reason refers to a specific value and its relation to all elements (including premoral evils) in the action [83]. The specific value in legalizing medical marijuana is to relieve pain and suffering associated with treatment for life-threatening illnesses. The premoral evil, which can come about by trying to achieve this value, is the foreseen but unintended possibility of the potential harmful effects of the smoke and the possibility that some may view this as condoning and even encouraging illegal drug use. The ethical question is: does the value of relieving pain and suffering outweigh the premoral evil of the potential harmful effects of the smoke and the possibility of scandal? To determine if a proper relationship exists between the specific value and the other elements of the act, ethicist Richard McCormick proposes three criteria for the establishment of proportionate reason:

1. The means used will not cause more harm than necessary to achieve the value.
2. No less harmful way exists to protect the value.
3. The means used to achieve the value will not undermine it [84].

The application of McCormick's criteria to the legalization of medical marijuana supports the argument that there is a proportionate reason for allowing physicians to prescribe marijuana. First, the most comprehensive scientific analysis to date by the Institute of Medicine cautioned that the benefits of smoking marijuana were limited because the smoke itself is toxic, but recommended that it be given, on a short-term basis under close supervision, to patients who do not respond to other therapies. The possible damage to an individual's lungs is a legitimate health concern; however, the patients who would benefit from the smoked marijuana are suffering from cancer, AIDS, MS, etc. Many of these conditions are terminal and the treatments they are undergoing also have toxic effects--chemotherapy, radiation, the AIDS cocktail, etc. The point is that the benefit of the treatments outweighs the burdens. The focus should be on encouraging the federal government to direct its research resources toward the development of alternative methods of delivering cannabinoids in the form of patches, capsules and bronchial inhalers. In this way the toxicity could be eliminated. The Institute of Medicine study also reported that there was no evidence that prescribing medical marijuana would increase illicit drug use or that it is a "gateway drug" that prompts patients to use harder drugs like cocaine or heroin. Second, at present, there does not seem to be an alternative medication that is as effective as smoked marijuana. Thousands of patients who have smoked marijuana illegally for medical purposes have attested to its effectiveness. Those patients who were and are involved in the government sponsored compassionate care program also attest to smoked marijuana's effectiveness. In addition, scientific studies have shown that Marinol, Nabilone and Sativex are less effective, more difficult for nauseous patients to consume, and more expensive than smoked marijuana. There are also other approved antiemetic drugs or combinations of these drugs which have been shown to be effective in relieving pain and suffering in some cancer patients [85]. However, for others these medications have proven ineffective. To date, the only therapy that relieves their nausea and vomiting is smoking marijuana. Third, smoking marijuana for medical reasons does not undermine the value, which is the relief of pain and suffering. Many of the patients who would use medical marijuana are suffering from terminal conditions and are undergoing therapies that have serious side-effects. Since this seems to be the only therapy to date that relieves the pain and suffering of these patients, one can argue convincingly that it is a medical necessity. The federal government's concern that legalizing medical marijuana could lead to the possibility of the slippery slope in regards to drug use is a real fear. But, this has not occurred with other prescription psychoactive drugs (e.g., morphine, codeine, cocaine, etc.) and there is no evidence it would occur with marijuana. Therefore, it is ethically justified under the principle of double effect for the federal government to legalize marijuana for patients who do not respond to traditional therapies. Seriously ill patients have the right to effective therapies. To deny them access to such therapies is to deny them the dignity and respect all persons deserve. The greater good is promoted in spite of the potential evil consequences.

Conclusion

After reviewing pertinent scientific data, it is evident that there is ample evidence to warrant the Obama Administration to authorize the DEA to reclassify marijuana as a Schedule II drug, which would allow the drug to be used for medical purposes. As a candidate, President Obama promised to maintain a hands-off approach in the this matter and Attorney General Eric Holder also stated that federal prosecutors would not prosecute patients or providers in accordance with state law; however, recent crackdowns suggest otherwise [86]. In order to ensure the proper regulation of medical marijuana and the issues currently surrounding the topic, the following recommendations are proposed:

1. Government rescheduling of marijuana.

The top priority of the government, in regards to medical marijuana, should be to reclassify the drug as a Schedule II drug. This would enable dispensaries, clinics, pharmacies and physicians to provide patients with standardized, unadulterated forms of marijuana. If marijuana continues to be unregulated, patients will be forced to seek black-market marijuana, and risk possible legal repercussions to alleviate their condition. This argument is grounded in harm reduction, both legally and medically. Utilizing the proper legal and medical controls can provide an effective strategy to identify and reduce health hazards associated with smoked marijuana, as well as help to reduce legal prosecution faced with unregulated marijuana [87].

2. FDA regulation of medical marijuana growth.

Marijuana contains over 460 known compounds, sixty of which are cannabinoids. There are also a number of carcinogens present in smoked marijuana. The main psychoactive compound in the drug is THC, which controls the strength or potency. THC concentration in black-market marijuana can vary greatly, which can lead to adverse effects for patients who may seek alleviating effects for their condition. To minimize such health risks, the federal government, specifically the FDA, must monitor marijuana produced for medical purposes. Recently, there have been numerous crackdowns on people who grow marijuana for medical uses. This problem is therefore two-fold, with medical and legal aspects. If the FDA was to intervene and oversee the production of marijuana, this would reduce the number of questions surrounding the growing of marijuana and the arrests that follow, as well as control the hazardous aspects of marijuana. If FDA regulation is present in medical marijuana production, the THC concentration and concentration of other hazardous compounds in marijuana can be controlled, thus reducing the harmful effects that impact the health of numerous patients.

3. Advance research into more pure forms of smoked marijuana and cost effective alternatives.

The medical community has provided studies proving the efficacy of marijuana in treatment of patients who have not responded to other treatments. Specifically, these studies have shown the therapeutic value of marijuana in controlling pain, alleviating nausea and vomiting, as well as alleviating symptoms of multiple sclerosis (MS) and AIDS. In 2011, a randomized controlled trial of cannabinoids' treatment of chronic non-cancer pain also demonstrated positive outcomes [56]. Significant analgesic effects were seen in treating neuropathic pain, fibromyalgia, and rheumatoid arthritis. The most effective cannabinoid available to patients is smoked marijuana, however due to varying THC concentrations and the fact that the mode of ingestion is inhaled smoke, there are also adverse effects. Two options that may help to reduce these adverse effects are more pure forms of smoked marijuana and cost effective alternatives. A more pure form of smoked marijuana (i.e., less toxic compounds) would reduce the harmful effects of smoked marijuana, and therefore increase the benefits. Cannabinoid alternatives reduce the amount of these harmful compounds in marijuana. Such alternatives like Marinol, Nabilone, and Sativex do exist, however the two concerns that these alternatives pose are efficacy and cost. Smoked marijuana continues to be substantially more effective than these alternatives, and the cost of smoked marijuana is significantly less. In order to improve these alternatives and create new options, more research is needed.

4. Increased funding enabling agencies to accomplish this research.

Medical marijuana research is contingent upon National Institutes of Health (NIH) funding. For 2011, the NIH has allocated only $2 million in the form of 4-5 grants for research in marijuana [88]. In order to properly research safer and cost effective alternatives, more NIH funding is necessary, and must be done to provide suffering patients with a beneficial treatment.

5. Increased pharmaceutical research into new medical marijuana alternatives (i.e., marijuana patch, inhaler, etc.).

To advance the development of new marijuana treatment alternatives, pharmaceutical companies should be given incentives to continue to explore new avenues for suffering patients. One such company that has begun development on a medical marijuana patch is Medical Marijuana Delivery Systems (MMDS) LLC. In February 2011, MMDS announced that they had acquired United States Patent rights to develop a marijuana patch for medical use. Walter Cristobal, the patch inventor, is working with MMDS to develop the patch-based delivery, as well as other delivery systems like creams and gels [43]. Another recent development in the marijuana industry has come from the pharmaceutical company Medicinal Genomics. As of August 2011, the company has successfully sequenced the entire genome of the cannabis plant, a breakthrough which has the potential to grow the number of treatment options available to patients [89].

Ethically speaking, denying physicians the right to prescribe a therapy that relieves pain and suffering to their patients is a violation of the physician-patient relationship. Patients are entitled to full disclosure of all possible treatment options from their physician in order to make an informed medical decision regarding their health. It is the medical responsibility of a physician to offer adequate relief from pain for their patients so that the patient may have an acceptable quality of life. Failure to provide an available therapy that has been proven effective would violate the basic ethical principle of beneficence, which is the obligation of physicians to seek the well-being or benefit of the patient. Under beneficence, a physician's duties include preventing and removing harm, as well as promoting the good of their patient. To allow a patient to suffer when an effective treatment is available is to directly harm the patient, and therefore a violation of beneficence. Scientific research has shown that the benefits of medical marijuana greatly outweigh the burdens.

Overall, all people, especially in the federal government and the medical field, should be concerned over the quality of life of those suffering from neurological and movement disorders, cancer, wasting syndrome attributable to AIDS, etc. A 2010 Gallup poll of Americans has shown significant support for making marijuana legally available for doctors to prescribe for patients. The poll found that seventy percent of Americans are in favor, as negative feelings continue to decline [89]. Medical marijuana has proven invaluable in the battle against terminal illnesses; however, unless the federal government publically acknowledges this fact, numerous terminal patients will continue to suffer needlessly.

The fight against drug abuse is important because may lives are lost to drug addiction, but the effects of devastating illnesses impacts a substantially greater number of Americans. Medical marijuana can be an important treatment for physicians to confront the challenges of patients' pain and suffering. The apparent political motivations present in the federal government must be eliminated because the quality of numerous American lives hangs in the balance. The dignity and respect of all persons must be a priority for the Obama Administration. It is time to voice support for the most vulnerable and reclassify medical marijuana as a Schedule II drug, because for many patients it is truly a medical necessity.

REFERENCES

[1] Jonas WB. Alternative medicine – Learning from the Past, Examining the Present, Advancing to the Future. *Journal of the American Medical Association 280*. 11 Nov. 1998: 1616.

[2] Annas GJ. Reefer Madness – The Federal Response to California's Medical-Marijuana Law. *The New England Journal of Medicine 337*. 7 Aug. 1997: 439.

[3] National Conference of State Legislatures, "State Medical Marijuana Laws," November 11, 2015. http://www.nesl.org/research/health/state/state-medical-marijuana-laws.aspx.

[4] Stack P, Suddath C. A brief history of medical marijuana. *Time*. 21 Oct. 2009. Available from: http://www.time.com/time/health/article/0,8599,1931247,00.html.

[5] Webley K. Brief History: Medical Marijuana. *Time*. 21 Jun. 2010, Vol. 175 Issue 24, p22.

[6] Thomas J. The Past Present, and Future of Medical Marijuana in the United States. *Psychiatric Times*. 6 Jan. 2010, Vol. 27 No. 1. Available from: http://www.psychiatrictimes.com/display/article/10168/1507650.

[7] Federal Drug Classification Schedules. *National Substance Abuse Index*. 2006. Available from: http://nationalsubstanceabuseindex.org/drugclass.htm.

[8] Johnson K. In Montana, A Bid to End Medical Use of Marijuana. *The New York Times*. 10 Feb. 2011. Available from: http://www.nytimes.com/2011/02/11/us/11marijuana.html?ref=kirkjohnson.

[9] Carpenter E. Judge: Anaheim can ban medical pot shops. *OCRegister.com*. 22 Aug. 2011. Available from: http://articles.ocregister.com/2011-08-22/news/29920039_1_anaheim-s-law-appeals-court-california-s-4th-district-court.

[10] 10 States with Pending Legislation to Legalize Medical Marijuana. 13 May 2011. Available from: http://medicalmarijuana.procon.org/view.resource.php?resourceID=002481.

[11] Delaware legalizes medical marijuana. *Reuters*. 13 May 2011. Available from: http://www.reuters.com/article/2011/05/13/us-delaware-legalizes-medical-marijuana-idUSTRE74C6X120110513.

[12] Carpenter M. PA bill would legalize marijuana as therapeutic option. *Pittsburgh Post-Gazette*. 11 Jul. 2010. Available from: http://www.post-gazette.com/pg/10192/1072041-51.stm.

[13] Stempsey WE. The Battle for Medical Marijuana in the War on Drugs. *America 23*. 11 Apr. 1998: 14.

[14] Gay Stolberg S. For a Very Few Patients, U.S. Provides Free Marijuana. *The New York Times*. 19 Mar. 1999: A-10.

[15] Gay Stolberg S. Government Study on Marijuana Sees Medical Benefits. *The New York Times*. 18 Mar. 1999: A1. See also, Joy JE, Watson SJ, Jr., Benson JA. Marijuana And Medicine: Assessing The Science Base. *Washington, D.C.: Institute of Medicine*. Mar. 1999: 99.

[16] Joy et al., 3.

[17] Ibid., 438. The following findings must be made to place a drug on Schedule I: "(A) The drug… has a high potential for abuse; (B) The drug… has no currently accepted medical use in treatment in the United States; and (C) there is a lack of accepted safety for use of the drug under medical supervision." Part A for a Schedule II drug is identical; the other requirements are "(B) The drug… has currently accepted medical use in the United States; and (C) Abuse of the drug… may lead to severe psychological and physical dependence." Ibid.

[18] Should marijuana be a medical option? 7 Jun. 2011. Available from: http://medicalmarijuana.procon.org/.

[19] Szalavitz M. U.S. Rules that Marijuana has no Medical Use. What Does Science Say? *Time*. 11 Jul. 2011. Available from: http://healthland.time.com/2011/07/11/u-s-rules-marijuana-has-no-medical-use-what-does-science-say/?artId=38018?contType=article?chn=us.

[20] Grinspoon L, Bakalar JB. Marijuana, the Forbidden Medicine. New Haven, CT: *Yale University Press*. 1993: 1-2.

[21] United States of America. United States Department of Health and Human Services. *Investigating Possible Medical Uses of Marijuana*. 25 Mar. 1999: 1-2.

[22] Medical Marijuana and the Mind. *Harvard Health Publications - Harvard Medical School*. Apr. 2010. Available from: http://www.health.harvard.edu/newsletters/Harvard_Mental_Health_Letter/2010/April/medical-marijuana-and-the-mind.

[23] For a more detailed analysis, see, Rachelfsky GS, Opedz G. Normal Lymphocyte Function in the Presence of Delta-9-THC. *Clinical Pharmacology Therapy*. 1977: 44-46.; Cabral GA, Fisher-Stenger K. Inhibition of Macrophage Inducible Protein Expression by Delta-9-THC. *Life Sciences 54*. 1994: 1831-44.; Zhu W, Newton C, Daaka Y, et al., Delta-9-tetrahydrocannabinol Enhances the Secretion on Interleukin I from Edotoxin Stimulated Macrophages. *Journal of Pharmacological Experimental Therapy 270*. 1994: 1334-39.

[24] McPartland JM, Pruitt P. Medical Marijuana and Its Use by the Immunocompromised. *Alternative Therapies 3*. May 1997: 41.

[25] Ibid., 41-42.

[26] Ibid., 42-43.

[27] Marmor B. Medical Marijuana. *Western Journal of Medicine 168*. 1998: 542. See also, Devane WA, Hanus L, Breuer A, et al., Isolation and Structure of a Brain Constituent that Binds to the Cannabinoid Receptor. *Science 258*. 1992: 1946-49.

[28] McPartland: 39. It should be noted that the DEA has rejected proposed protocols accepted by the FDA. "The Clinical trial devised by D.I. Abrams et al., has been approved by the FDA (as well as the California Research Advisory Panel, the institutional review board of the University of California, and the scientific advisory board of the San Francisco Community Consortium). Unfortunately, the protocol was rejected by the DEA and the National Institute of Drug Abuse. Political disingenuity involved in this rejection has frustrated members of Congress" (Ibid. 39-40). Five years later, Dr. Abrams of the University of California at San Francisco finally obtained approval and a $978,000 National Institutes of Health grant. "Even then, Dr. Abrams said he had to mask his true research interest. Although he wanted to examine the effects of marijuana on the weight loss associated with AIDS, he pitched the study as one that would look at potentially toxic interactions between marijuana and standard AIDS medications. 'We designed a study that would appeal to the group of people funding the grant.' " Gay Stolberg

S. Restrictions Ease for Studies on Marijuana as Medicine. *The New York Times*. 22 May 1999: A-11.

[29] National Institutes of Health (NIH) – Budget. 2010.

[30] United States of America. United States Government – Department of Health and Human Services. *Medical Marijuana Policy Research: Exploring Trends and Impacts (R01)*. 29 Oct. 2010. Available from: http://grants.nih.gov/grants/guide/rfa-files/RFA-DA-11-008.html.

[31] United States of America. United States Department of Health and Human Services, 2.

[32] Marinol may be taken anywhere from 2 to 6 times per day depending on a person's needs (Dronabinol PubMed Health).

[33] Stolberg. Restrictions Ease For Studies On Marijuana As Medicine: A-11.

[34] Dubb T. Why marinol cannot substitute for marijuana. *MD Safe Access Now*. 8 Jan. 2009. Available from: http://mdsafeaccess.blogspot.com/2009/01/why-marinol-cannot-substitute-for.html.

[35] Gwynne P. Medical Marijuana Debate moving Towards Closure. *The Scientist* 7. 18 Mar. 1997: 1.

[36] Ware MA, St Arnaud-Trempe E. The abuse potential of the synthetic cannabinoid nabilone. *Addiction*. Mar 2010. Vol. 105 Issue 3: p494-503.

[37] Gever J. Marijuana Derivative Called Effective in Fibromyalgia. *MedPage Today*. 15 Feb. 2008. Available from: http://www.medpagetoday.com/Rheumatology/Fibromyalgia/8377.

[38] Koch W. Spray alternative to pot on the market in Canada. *USA Today*. 23 June 2005. Available from: http://www.usatoday.com/news/health/2005-06-23-pot-spray_x.htm.

[39] Kavia RB, DeRidder D, Constantinescu CS, Stott CG, Fowler CJ. Randomized controlled trial of Sativex to treat detrusor overactivity in multiple sclerosis. London, UK: National Hospital for Neurology and Neurosurgery. *Mult Scler*. 2010 Nov; 16(11): 1349-59. *Epub* 9 Sept. 2010.

[40] Peat S. Using cannabinoids in pain and palliative care. I*nternational Journal of Palliative Nursing*. Oct 2010. Vol. 16 Issue 10: p481-485, 5p.

[41] Cooper R. GW Pharmaceuticals launches world's first prescription cannabis drug in Britain. *The Telegraph*. 21 Jun. 2010.

[42] Marmor: 541. See also, Adams IB, Martin BR. Cannabis: Pharmacology and Toxicology in Animals and Humans. *Addiction 91*. 1996: p1585-1614.

[43] MMDS Acquires Patent for Medical Marijuana Patch. *PR Newswire*. 22 Feb. 2011. Available from: http://www.prnewswire.com/news-releases/mmds-acquires-patent-for-medical-marijuana-patch-116647604.html.
[44] Annas: 438. See also, Doblin RE, Kleiman MA. Marijuana as Antiemetic Medicine: A Survey of Oncologists' Experiences and Attitudes. *Journal of Clinical Oncology 9*. 1991: 1314-19.
[45] Grinspoon and Bakalar: 150.
[46] Van Grinsven J, Westerik H. Medicinal use of cannabis: A report [in Dutch]. Utrecht, Netherlands. *Duo Market Research*. 2003.
[47] Stolberg. For a Very Few Patients, U.S. Provides Free Marijuana: A-10.
[48] United States of America. National Institute of Drug Abuse, Report to the Director. National Institutes of Health. Bethesda, MD. *Workshop on the Medical Utility of Marijuana*. 1997.
[49] Stolberg. Government Study Of Marijuana Sees medical Benefits: A-1, A-19.
[50] Shrivastava A, Kuzontkoski PM, Groopman JE, Prasad A. Cannabidiol Induces Programmed Cell Death in Breast Cancer Cells by Coordinating the Cross-talk between Apoptosis and Autophagy. *Mol. Cancer Ther.*, Jul. 2011; 10(7): 1161-72.
[51] Vara D, Salazar M, Olea-Herrero N, Guzmán M, Velasco G, Díaz-Laviada I. Anti-tumoral action of cannabinoids on hepatocellular carcinoma: role of AMPK-dependent activation of autophagy. *Cell Death Differ*. Jul. 2011; 18(7): 1099-111.
[52] Ruhaak LR, Felth J, Karlsson PC, Rafter JJ, Verpoorte R, Bohlin L. Evaluation of the cyclooxygenase inhibiting effects of six major cannabinoids isolated from Cannabis sativa. *Biol. Pharm Bull*. 2011; 34(5): 774-8.
[53] Roser P, Vollenweider FX, Kawohl W. Potential antipsychotic properties of central cannabinoid (CB1) receptor antagonists. *World J. Biol. Psychiatry*. Mar. 2010; 11(2 Pt 2): 208-19.
[54] Howes MJ, Perry E. The role of phytochemicals in the treatment and prevention of dementia. *Drugs Aging*. 1 Jun. 2011; 28(6): 439-68.
[55] Sagredo O, Pazos MR, Satta V, Ramos JA, Pertwee RG, Fernández-Ruiz J. Neuroprotective effects of phytocannabinoid-based medicines in experimental models of Huntington's disease. *J. Neurosci. Res*. Sept. 2011; 89(9): 1509-18.
[56] Lynch ME, Campbell F. Cannabinoids for Treatment of Chronic Non-Cancer Pain; a Systematic Review of Randomized Trials. *Br. J. Clin. Pharmacol*. Nov 2011; 72(5): 735-44.

[57] Ogden DW. Investigations and Prosecutions in States Authorizing the Medical Use of Marijuana. *Memorandum for Selected United States Attorneys*. Oct. 2009. Available from: http://www.justice.gov/opa/documents/medical-marijuana.pdf.
[58] Yardley W. New Federal Crackdown Confounds States That Allow Medical Marijuana. *The New York Times*. 7 May 2011. Available from: http://www.nytimes.com/2011/05/08/us/08marijuana.html?pagewanted=all.
[59] Fudge T. Medical Marijuana Arrests; Calif. Isn't Mellow Yet. *NPR*. 19 Sept. 2009. Available from: http://www.npr.org/templates/story/story.php?storyId=112961966.
[60] Hoeffel J. U.S. decrees that marijuana has no accepted medical use. *Los Angeles Times*. 9 Jul. 2011.
[61] Lantis NT. California, Arizona Laws Permit medical Use of Marijuana. *American Journal of Health System Pharmacy 54*. 15 Jan. 1997: 126.
[62] Kocieniewski D. New Jersey Vote Backs Marijuana for Severely Ill. *The New York Times*. 11 Jan. 2010.
[63] Beginning in 1969 with President Nixon, the United States engaged in a national "war on drugs" culminating in the enactment of the Controlled Substances Act, discussed herein.
[64] 84 Stat. 1248.
[65] *See* Delaware Division of Corporations, http://www.corp.delaware.gov/aboutagency.shtml, noting that 63% of the Fortune 500 have chosen Delaware as their legal home.
[66] *See generally, Gonzalez v. Raich*, 545 U.S. 1 (2005). Unless otherwise cited, all factual and legal citations concerning that case are derived from the Supreme Court's opinion.
[67] Cal. Health & Safety Code Ann. § 11362.5 (West Supp. 2005).
[68] *Raich*, 545 U.S. at 6 (citing the Compassionate Use Act).
[69] At the time the case commenced, John Ashcroft was the Attorney General. By the time the case reached the Supreme Court, Alberto Gonzalez was the Attorney General and, thus, the named party in the lawsuit.
[70] *Raich v. Ashcroft*, 248 F. Supp. 2d 918 (N.D. Cal. 2003).
[71] *Raich v. Ashcroft*, 352 F.3d 1222 (9th Cir. 2003).
[72] Article I, Section 8, Clause 3.
[73] That case, *Wickard v. Filburn*, involved a farmer who grew 23 acres of wheat at a time when government regulations permitted each farmer to grow only 11.1 acres, in an effort to avoid surpluses and abnormally low

prices. The farmer, Filburn, argued that he intended to personally consume the surplus and it therefore did not affect interstate commerce, but the Supreme Court rejected his argument, holding that while his personal use may have been trivial, the aggregate affect of others similarly situated, was far from trivial and has a substantial affect on interstate commerce. *See* 317 U.S. 111 (1942).

[74] Article VI, Clause 2.

[75] Mangan J. An Historical Analysis of The Principle Of Double Effect. *Theological Studies* 10. Mar. 1949: 41.

[76] Kelly G. Medico-Moral Problems. St. Louis, MO: *The Catholic Health Association of the United States and Canada*. 1958: 13-14.

[77] It should be noted that some might argue that smoking marijuana by itself, independently of its effects, is morally evil. This implies that certain actions in themselves are intrinsically evil and to do them is always morally wrong. However, when one enters the realm of a "moral" action, one is speaking of an action qualified by intention and circumstances. So unqualified actions can only be called "premoral actions." For a more detailed analysis, see Gula RM. *Reason Informed By Faith: Foundations Of Catholic Morality*. New York: Paulist Press; 1989: 270-271. Premoral evil refers to the lack of perfection in anything whatsoever. As pertaining to human actions, it is that aspect that we experience as regrettable, harmful, or detrimental to the full actualization of the well-being of persons and of their social relationships. For a more detailed description, see Janssens L. Ontic Evil and Moral Evil. *Readings in Moral Theology, No. 1: Moral Norms And Catholic Tradition*, ed. Curran CF and McCormick RA. Ramsey (NJ): Paulist Press; 1979: 60.

[78] Annas, 437.

[79] Stempsey, 16.

[80] Annas, 438. See also, Wren C. Phantom Numbers Haunt the War on Drugs. *New York Times*. 20 Apr. 1997: E-4.

[81] Van Ours JC. Is Cannabis a Stepping-Stone for Cocaine. *Journal of Health Economics* 22. 2003: 539-554.

[82] Annas, 438.

[83] Walter JJ. Proportionate Reason and Its Three Levels Of Inquiry: Structuring The Ongoing Debate. *Louvain Studies* 10. Spring 1984: 32.

[84] McCormick's criteria for proportionate reason first appeared in McCormick R, *Ambiguity in Moral Choice*. Milwaukee (WI): Marquette University Press, 1973. He later reworked the criteria in response to

criticism. His revised criteria can be found in *Doing Evil to Achieve Good*, eds. McCormick R, Ramsey P. Chicago (IL): Loyola University Press, 1978.

[85] Examples include drugs called serotonin antagonists which include ondansetron (Zofran) and granisetron (Kytril), used alone or combined with dexamethasone (a steroid hormone); metoclopramide (Reglan) combined with diphenhydramine and dexamethasone; high doses of methylprednisolone (a steroid hormone) combined with droperidol (Inapsine); and prochlorperazine (Compazine). National Institute on Drug Abuse, 2.

[86] Obama Not Implicated In California Medical Marijuana Crackdown, U.S. Attorney Claims. *Huffington Post*. 26 Oct. 2011. Available from: http://www.huffingtonpost.com/2011/10/26/obama-administration-medical-marijuana-crackdown-california_n_1033482.html.

[87] McPartland & Pruitt: 44.

[88] United States of America. Department of Health and Human Services. *Medical marijuana policy research: exploring trends and impacts (R01)*. 29 Oct. 2010. Available from: http://grants.nih.gov/grants/guide/rfa-files/RFA-DA-11-008.html.

[89] Mendes E. New high of 46% of Americans support legalizing marijuana. *Gallup Poll*. 28 Oct. 2010. Available from: http://www.gallup.com/poll/144086/New-High-Americans-Support-Legalizing-Marijuana.aspx.

In: Marijuana
Editor: Margie Vasquez
ISBN: 978-1-63484-409-3

Chapter 3

The Effects of Marijuana Legalization on Public Health and Usage among College-Age Young Adults

Teminijesu Ige**, Bradley Fevrier and Laura Nabors
Health Promotion and Education Program, University of Cincinnati, Cincinnati, Ohio, US

Abstract

The use of marijuana has been a controversial issue since the early 20th century when regulation and restriction on its use began to take hold, culminating in its classification as a Schedule I controlled substance under the 1970 Comprehensive Drug Abuse Prevention and Control Act (Controlled Substances Act), and hence its prohibition in the United States. However, studies on marijuana have shown some evidence for beneficial medical use of the substance. These medical uses include the treatment of acute and chronic pain, symptomatic relief in AIDS, and treatment of cancer, mental illness and addiction among others.

Nevertheless marijuana, like numerous other pharmacologic substances, has its documented adverse effects including hallucinations, short-term memory and learning deficits, loss of coordination, increased risk of respiratory tract and other cancers, and increased tendency to use

---

* E-mail addresses: igetm@mail.uc.edu naborsla@ucmail.uc.edu.

other dangerous and addictive substances such as cocaine. Furthermore, there have been major concerns expressed by opponents over the state-level legalization of medical marijuana with the view that legalization will make the drug more appealing and readily accessible to young adults (college-age students), thereby worsening the existing public health problem.

This review of literature examines the evidence for and against the medical use of marijuana, and the effects and implications of its recent legalization in several states especially with regard to its use by college-age young adults. The findings of this review will provide information that will have the potential to contribute to the development of policies that will better protect the health and well-being of college students and allow for the development of prevention messages and interventions to serve this vulnerable group.

Introduction

The purpose of this chapter is to discuss marijuana as it relates to college-age young adult use in the context of the present efforts to legalize marijuana in the United States. We will define marijuana misuse, highlight prevalence and trends in marijuana use especially among college age young adults (18-24 years), discuss the medical uses of marijuana, examine the health risks (hazards) of marijuana misuse and describe the high risk groups for marijuana use. We will also look at the effects of legalization of marijuana on its use, risks for use among college-age young adults in states where marijuana is legalized, prevention messages that can be employed to protect young people, and interventions that have been carried out to reduce the adverse effects of marijuana use.

Defining Marijuana Misuse

Since its classification as a Schedule I controlled substance in 1970, marijuana became an illicit drug and any use of the drug was deemed misuse and declared illegal. More recently, as the medicinal properties of the plant have become more recognized, a distinction is being made between marijuana use for medicinal purposes and use for non-medicinal or recreational purposes (Budney and Stanger 2012). Even though any use (medicinal or non-medicinal) can produce adverse effects, non-medicinal or recreational use, being unregulated, is usually more associated with adverse effects and higher potential for abuse or dependence (Hoch et al., 2015). Marijuana misuse can therefore be defined as illicit non-medicinal use of the substance which is potentially harmful, but does not fulfill the Diagnosis and Statistical Manual of Mental Disorders (DSM-IV) criteria for abuse or dependence (Menghrajani et al., 2005). Abuse and dependence as defined by the DSM-IV both feature the presence of a maladaptive pattern of use which results in clinically identifiable and substantial adverse health effects (Center for Substance Abuse Treatment 2004). It is important to note that even though there is a high potential for marijuana misuse to progress to abuse or addiction, this transition does not always occur (Budney and Stanger 2012).

Still, the negative consequences commonly attributed to marijuana misuse present a legitimate public health problem that requires consideration and action aimed at developing systems that are more effective in treatment and prevention interventions. Studies have shown that prolonged misuse of marijuana, especially in adolescence, is responsible for less well-organized neural processing on tasks necessitating executive functioning, especially those tasks that require a greater degree of control or attention (Abdullaev et al., 2010). In the same way, regular marijuana use among teens, and early onset of marijuana use have been thought to be linked with less proficient cognitive processing on working memory tasks (Becker et al., 2010; Jager et al., 2010; Schweinsburg et al., 2010).

In most cases, the structure and experience of marijuana (cannabis) use disorders is relatively comparable to what has been observed with other substance use disorders (Budney 2006). Studies have shown that most adults who misuse marijuana, and as a result have to seek treatment, have on average been using marijuana daily for about a decade (Budney 2006; Budney et al., 2007; Copeland et al., 2001; Stephens et al., 2002). It is also note-worthy that most of these users have made numerous unsuccessful attempts at quitting. Their experiences are marked by a vast array of misuse, abuse and dependence symptoms. Dependence manifests as continued marijuana use notwithstanding the negative social, psychological and sometimes physical issues that occur as a result of its use. Marijuana addicts have perceptions of an inability to refrain from using the drug and even when they do actually stop, most people experience withdrawal symptoms as a result of the abrupt cessation. Additionally, people who misuse marijuana acknowledge that the adverse effects negatively affect their family relationships resulting in guilt which leads to more psychological problems. Financial complications, low energy level, unhappiness with efficiency level, sleep and memory problems, and low life satisfaction and self-esteem are all additional consequences of marijuana misuse (Stephens et al., 2002).

Prevalence and Trends in Marijuana Use among College-Age Young Adults

In the United States (US) there are 24.6 million illicit drug users, which is 9.4 percent of the country's population aged 12 years or older, according to the 2013 National Survey on Drug Use and Health (Substance Abuse and Mental Health Services Administration (SAMHSA) 2014). The survey also revealed that marijuana is the most widely used illicit substance in the US. In 2013, 81% (19.8 million) of illicit drug users older than 12 years admitted to having used it within the past 30 days of responding to the survey. This total number of marijuana users (19.8 million) represents 7.5% of the US population and an increase of 1.7% (4.5 million new users) from the figures provided in 2007. Additionally, the data from the National Survey on Drug Use and Health (NSDUH) has shown a steady increase in marijuana use among the general population over the age of 12 years, from 5.8% in 2007 (19.8 million users) to 7.4% in 2013. On the other hand, the use of other illicit drugs (cocaine, hallucinogens and psychotherapeutics) has declined over the same period. Thus marijuana is the single responsible factor for the net rise in illicit drug use over the past five years.

The increased rate of marijuana use is also reflected among college-age young adults (ages 18-25 years) in the United States. Among this population, marijuana use increased from approximately 16-17% (2002-2008) to approximately 18-19% (2009-2012), and then was about 19% of all illicit drug users in 2013. Also, according to the NSDUH, the average age at which people initiated marijuana use in 2013 was 18.0 years (SAMHSA 2014). Salas-Wright et al., (2015) analyzed the NSDUH (2002-2013) and found that, among people aged 12-25, young adults (aged 18-25) had the highest rate of self-reported life-time marijuana use (about 52%) compared to older adolescents aged 15-17 years (about 29%) and younger adolescents aged 12-14 years (about 6%). Furthermore, it was discovered that initiation of marijuana use as a young adult between the ages of 18 and 25 years was more associated with dependence or abuse than initiation at an older age (SAMHSA 2014).

MEDICAL USES OF MARIJUANA

Most of the popularity associated with the use of marijuana has come from its recreational properties which are due to its ability to alter sensory perception and cause ecstasy and exhilaration. However, the medicinal properties of the plant resulting from chemicals which are structurally and functionally analogous to the human endocannabinoid system, are also widely known. A full discussion of the established and potential medical uses of marijuana is beyond the scope of this chapter, therefore this section will focus on medical uses for which there are Food and Drug Administration (FDA)-approved medications or medications currently undergoing clinical trials. Some other promising medical uses will also be mentioned. In order to facilitate understanding of the medicinal properties of marijuana, the endocannabinoid system will be briefly described and the marijuana-derived cannabinoids will be identified.

The Endocannabinoid System

The endocannabinoid system refers to a group of receptors, lipids (cannabinoids) and enzymes that are present naturally throughout the human body, especially within the nervous and immune systems (Grotenhermen and Müller-Vahl 2012). There are two main receptors that have been identified as part of the endocannabinoid system – Cannabinoid receptor type 1 (CB_1) and Cannabinoid receptor type 2 (CB_2). CB_1 which is mostly found in the Central Nervous System but also in numerous other peripheral organs and tissues is responsible for the psychotropic (mind-altering) properties of the endocannabinoid system. CB_2 on the other hand is mostly expressed by cells of the immune system and is mainly responsible for the medical properties (Grotenhermen and Müller-Vahl 2012). There are other receptors, such as the vanilloid-1 receptor, which play a less prominent role but which are important nonetheless. These receptors all form the first component of the endocannabinoid system. The second component, the lipids (cannabinoids), which include anandamide, 2-arachidonoyl glycerol (2-AG), noladin ether, virodhamine, N-arachidonoyl-dopamine (NADA) and others, act as messengers which transmit messages by binding to the receptors (Shoemaker et al., 2005; Bisogno et al., 2000). These cannabinoids are called *endogenous cannabinoids* (endocannabinoids) because they are naturally present within the human body. They are similar in structure to those found in the marijuana plant (*exogenous cannabinoids* or exocannabinoids), and this explains many of the effects of marijuana as will be discussed later in this section. The third component, the enzymes – including fatty acid amide hydrolase – are responsible for producing and removing the lipids (cannabinoids), thus maintaining a balance in the endocannabinoid system (Pazos et al., 2005).

Marijuana-Derived Cannabinoids

The marijuana plant contains more than 100 cannabinoids which, due to their structural and functional similarity to endogenous cannabinoids, all play a part in producing the effects that marijuana has on humans by binding to receptors of the endocannabinoid system (National Institutes of Health (NIH), 2015). However, there are two cannabinoids which have been most recognized for their medical properties – delta-9-tetrahydrocannabinol (THC) and Cannabidiol (CBD). THC has been identified as the main cannabinoid that binds with the CB1 receptor to produce the psychotropic (mind-altering) effects associated with marijuana use. CBD on the other hand blocks the CB1 receptor, stimulates the vanilloid-1 receptor and prevents the breakdown of one of the major endogenous cannabinoids – anandamide. It has been observed to play a major role in the beneficial medical properties associated with marijuana – reduction of pain and inflammation, symptomatic treatment of Acquired Immune Deficiency Syndrome (AIDS), seizure control, treatment of certain diseases of the nervous system, and treatment of some types of cancer (Grotenhermen and Müller-Vahl 2012; NIH 2015).

Presently, only two medications containing cannabinoids (THC and CBD) are currently approved by the Food and Drug Administration (FDA). These medications are Dronabinol and Nabilone which are used to treat nausea caused by cancer chemotherapy and to increase appetite in patients with extreme weight loss caused by AIDS. In addition to these, two drugs are currently being considered for approval for medical use – Nabiximols (Sativex) which treats muscle control problems caused by Multiple Sclerosis, and Epidiolex which is used in the treatment of certain types of childhood epilepsy (NIH 2015). With the decriminalization and legalization of marijuana in some states in the US, further research may reveal or establish other possible medical uses of marijuana.

Treatment of Pain

Records from countries such as China, India, Israel, Greece and Rome show that one of marijuana's earliest uses was to treat pain (Mechoulam and Hanus 2000). THC and CBD have both been proven to effectively reduce acute chemical, mechanical or thermal pain and have also been found to significantly alleviate chronic pain (Pacher et al., 2006). Furthermore, the pain-reducing effects have been observed to be more prominent when these cannabinoids are used in conjunction with other analgesics such as opioids and nonsteroidal anti-inflammatory drugs (Guindon et al., 2006; Manzanares et al., 2006). The anti-nociceptive (pain-reducing) effects have made exogenous cannabinoids useful in the treatment of pain related to chronic disease conditions such as Multiple Sclerosis, diabetic neuropathy, post-herpetic neuralgia and fibromyalgia (Manzanares et al., 2006).

Symptomatic Relief in AIDS

AIDS is often characterized by nausea and vomiting, loss of appetite (anorexia) and severe weight loss (cachexia). Marijuana-derived cannabinoids have been found to be very helpful with treating these symptoms. The anti-emetic (nausea and vomiting preventing) effect of Dronabinol was found to be comparable to standard anti-emetics such as prochlorperazine and metoclopramide, and was further found to have an additive effect when used in low doses in combination with standard anti-emetics (Grotenhermen and Müller-Vahl 2012). Furthermore Dronabinol has been found to reduce weight loss in AIDS patients through two mechanisms – improving appetite by modulating gastrointestinal motility and secretion, and directly influencing weight gain by affecting energy metabolism within the body (Grotenhermen and Müller-Vahl 2012; Pacher et al., 2006).

Cancer Treatment

Many types of cancer often manifest with pain, loss of appetite and weight, and sometimes nausea and vomiting especially during chemotherapy or radiotherapy. Therefore, the pain-reducing, appetite-stimulating and anti-emetic effects of exogenous cannabinoid medications such as Dronabinol have been found to be useful in the symptomatic treatment of cancer (Pacher et al.,

2006; NIH 2015). However, beyond symptomatic treatment, cannabinoids have been shown to be useful in fighting cancer. Studies have suggested that cannabinoids can directly inhibit cancer growth through the induction of cancer cell apoptosis (self-death), through anti-proliferative action, and through inhibition of angiogenesis (blood vessel formation) and tumor cell migration (Pacher et al., 2006; NIH 2015).

Treatment of Mental Illness and Addiction

The endocannabinoid system is heavily represented in the Central Nervous System (CNS) and it is therefore not surprising that cannabinoids exert a substantial influence in this system. Cannabinoids have been shown to affect the manifestation and progression of a wide range of illness associated with the CNS, including Alzheimer's disease, epilepsy, Amyotrophic Lateral Sclerosis (ALS), movement disorders such as Parkinson's disease and Huntington's disease, and Multiple Sclerosis (Pacher et al., 2006). In these illnesses, cannabinoids act through a wide range of mechanisms including reduction of inflammation, modulation of neuro-excitatory and neuro-inhibitory functions, reduction of neurotoxicity, and regulation of motor function. Beyond their role in the attenuation of pathological processes, cannabinoids have also been shown to play a role in the regulation of psychological functions. The well-known psychotropic properties of THC have found some use in the treatment of mental disorders such as schizophrenia, anxiety and depression, and insomnia. In addition, cannabinoids have been paradoxically found to possess the potential to help with the treatment of drug addiction and alcohol disorders. The mechanisms of this function have not been fully established and are still under investigation (Pacher et al., 2006).

Health Risks of Marijuana Use

The hazards or adverse health effects of marijuana have been a source of contention in debates about policies concerning the substance. Consequently, there have been many studies (epidemiological, clinical, and laboratory) that have linked certain adverse effects to marijuana use. For example, Hall (2009) suggested that there is strong enough evidence to conclude that marijuana use is associated with health risks that can adversely affect some users, particularly people who begin to use marijuana as adolescents and young adults who use it regularly. Some of these adverse effects include, but are not limited to, acute adverse reactions, increased risks of motor vehicle crashes, marijuana dependence, and psychotic symptoms. Marijuana use may also lead to long-term adverse results among adolescents, such as poorer educational outcomes and a greater likelihood of getting involved with other illicit drugs (Hall 2009).

Acute Adverse Effects of Marijuana Use

Acute adverse effects that have been associated with marijuana use include physiological effects such as increased heart rate (tachycardia), dry mouth (xerostomia), reddening of the eyes (conjunctival injection), reduction of the internal pressure of the eye (decreased intra-ocular pressure), and others. In addition psychological effects such as hallucinations and problems with short-term memory, verbal learning and attention have been observed. These effects are dose-related and depend on the method of administration (ingested or smoked) and user's previous experience (Hall and Degenhardt 2009). The acute toxicity of cannabinoids is marginal and they do not produce respiratory depression like the opioids (Gable 2004; Kalant 2004). According to Iverson (2008) and Gable (2004), the quantity of THC in laboratory experiments that kills rodents is relatively high and the assessed dosage that would be fatal to humans is measured to be between 15g and 70g. This would be much higher than what is usually smoked by heavy users (Gable, 2004).

Increased Risk of Vehicle Accidents

One of the greatest public health concerns of marijuana use is that marijuana-intoxicated drivers may contribute to motor vehicle crashes. According to Ramaekers et al., (2004), marijuana contributes to the reduction in cognitive and behavioral performance, which may in turn increase the risk of vehicle accidents by 2-3 times (Ramaekers et al., 2004). Also, Grotenhermen et al., (2007) and Gerberich et al., (2003) contend that many epidemiological studies have provided strong enough evidence that marijuana intoxicated drivers are at an increased risk of getting involved in motor vehicle crashes.

Increased Risk of Respiratory and Other Cancers

Mehra et al., (2006) conducted a systematic review of nineteen research studies to assess the impact of smoked marijuana on the risk for lung cancer among people aged 18 years and above. The case-control studies they analyzed revealed that there were more lung changes associated with a high risk for cancer in marijuana smokers compared with tobacco smokers and non-smokers. However, the observational studies that they analyzed showed no significant associations between marijuana smoking and the incidence of lung cancer, after adjusting for tobacco use. Also, Aldington et al., (2008) conducted a case-control study of lung cancer in adults aged 55 years and older. 79 people who had lung cancer and 324 people without lung cancer who acted as controls participated in the study. The researchers discovered that the risk of lung cancer increased 8% for each year of marijuana smoking, after adjusting for cigarette (tobacco) smoking. Other studies also confirm the increased risk of respiratory cancers associated with cannabis smoking (Voirin et al., 2006; Berthiller et al., 2008; Callaghan et al., 2013). Possible associations have also been found between marijuana use and other types of cancers including testicular cancer (Daling et al., 2009; Trabert et al., 2011; Lacson et al., 2012) and cancers of the head and neck (Hashibe et al., 2002; Goldenberg et al., 2004).

Risk of Addiction

There is reasonable evidence to indicate that prolonged exposure to the cannabinoids present in marijuana can eventually lead to addiction. According to Lopez-Quintero et al., (2001), about 9% of individuals who have experimented with marijuana will suffer from marijuana addiction/dependence based on the standards for dependence in the DSM-IV (Lopez-Quintero et al., 2001). It has been further suggested that the rate of addiction increases from approximately 16% (1 in 6) of experimental users who started marijuana use as teenagers to 25-50% among daily marijuana smokers (Hall and Degenhardt 2009). As has been previously mentioned, there is increased vulnerability and greater cause for concern with regard to long-term outcomes of marijuana use by adolescents (10-19 years). These adverse long-term outcomes are due the effects of exposure to exogenous cannabinoids on the ongoing development of the brain and the endocannabinoid system during this period (Mechoulam and Parker, 2013). According to Hall and Degenhardt (2007), early and consistent marijuana use significantly raises the risk of addiction, and marijuana addiction in turn eventually increases the risk of use of other illicit drugs. These findings were echoed by Chen et al., (2009) who suggested that, compared to individuals who began using marijuana as adults, there was approximately 2-4 times greater likelihood that those who began marijuana use as adolescents would suffer from marijuana dependence within two (2) years after initial use.

Effect on Brain Development

According to Gogtay et al., (2004), the brain is always in a constant active state of experience-guided development, an ongoing process that occurs from the prenatal phase through childhood and adolescence until about 21 years of age. Hence, during this developmental phase, the introduction of THC (one of the main active components of marijuana) is very detrimental for the developing child, adolescent and young adult. Gogtay et al., (2004) asserted that during childhood through early adulthood, the brain is intrinsically more susceptible to adverse long-term chemical exposure of any kind, thereby making it more vulnerable than the mature brain.

Relation to Mental Illness

Anxiety and depression have been identified as risk factors accompanying frequent marijuana use (Patton et al., 2002), but so far there has been no known proof of direct causality. Marijuana has also been associated with psychoses, particularly in people who possess pre-existing genetic susceptibility and recreational use may intensify the progression of illness in patients who suffer from schizophrenia (Caspi et al., 2005). More frequent marijuana use, superior drug strength (using very strong doses of the drug), and early exposure may all adversely impact mental disease progression (Di Forti et al., 2014). Nevertheless, despite the many studies on the subject, it is very difficult to prove that marijuana use actually causes any of the previously mentioned illnesses. Direct causality is difficult to prove because there are other confounding factors apart from marijuana use that may be possibly influential in the development of these mental illnesses.

Effects on Academic Performance of College-Age Students

Marijuana use may contribute to poor academic outcomes in the college years, if use begins during adolescence and is heavy in nature (Arria et al., 2015). Students who regularly use marijuana may often skip class and thus miss academic information, which further contributes to poor academic outcomes. Arria et al., examined the relationship between marijuana use, grade point average and time to graduation in a longitudinal study for over 1,000 college students. Additionally, variables related to psychological functioning and involvement in extracurricular activities were examined. Students were recruited as they entered college and participated in regular assessments of their substance use and academic performance for two to eight years. Findings of this study indicated that students who used marijuana in their first year of college were more likely to skip classes and in the long run and earn lower grades than those who did not use marijuana.

High Risk Factors for Marijuana Use among College Students

Among college-age young adults, several factors have been identified as predisposing them to marijuana use. The most influential factors include previous and/or concurrent use of other psychoactive substances (such as tobacco and alcohol), demographic factors (e.g., sex, and ethnic group), low educational achievement, unemployment, peer influences to use drugs, and adverse family situations. The role of each of these factors will be discussed below.

Use of Alcohol and Other Drugs

The previous and/or concurrent use of tobacco, alcohol and other psychoactive substances has been directly associated with the use of marijuana among young adults, either directly or through the influence of social networks. For instance, Cohn et al., (2015) found that current alcohol and marijuana use were associated with lifetime and past 30-day use of cigarettes, little cigars/cigarillos and hookah. Also Berg et al., (2015) discovered, among a sample of 2002 students at two colleges, that there were high concurrent rates of use of at least two psychoactive substances, with marijuana, hookah and e-cigarettes being the most frequently combined. In addition, Bonn-Miller and Zvolensky (2007) examined the factors that induce young adults to initiate marijuana use. They found that current levels of alcohol consumption and cigarette smoking predicted current and past 30-day marijuana use.

Demographic Factors

The risk for marijuana use is higher for males than females in the general population, and the gap between male and female use is widest during young adulthood (Pujazon-Zazik and Park 2009). According to the 2013 National Survey on Drug Use and Health (SAMHSA 2014), males were more likely than females to be current users of marijuana (9.7% versus 5.6% of the general population). The 2013 National Survey on Drug Use and Health (NSDUH) showed that the rate of illicit drug (including marijuana) use among the young adult population was 17.4% among persons reporting 2 or more races, 14.0% among Native Hawaiians or Other Pacific Islanders, 12.3% among American Indians or Alaska natives, 10.5% among Black Non-Hispanics, 9.5% among White Non-Hispanics, 8.8% among Hispanics and 3.1% among Asians.

Low Educational Achievement

Dropping out of school or college was found to be associated with an increased risk of illicit drug (including marijuana) use. The 2013 NSDUH (SAMHSA 2014) showed that college graduates had the least rate of illicit drug use (6.7%), compared with young adults with some college education but no degree (10.8%). On the other hand, young adults who graduated from high school with no further education had a rate of 9.9% compared to their peers who did not graduate (11.8%). The higher rates of illicit drug use in young adults who did not go on to higher education after high school showed that higher education is associated with less risk of being involved with illicit drugs. It is important to note that what causes use versus drop-out is a controversial question in many studies examining the relationship between these two factors. Further research is needed to understand what factors are related to low educational attainment that leads to marijuana use and similarly, to improve knowledge about what factors are related to marijuana use as a causative factors in dropping out of school. It is not yet fully understood if the same factors are related to each sequence of events.

Unemployment

Studies have shown that unemployment is associated with a higher risk of engaging in the use of marijuana (Hanson and Chen 2007; Redonnet et al., 2012). In confirmation of this fact, the 2013 NSDUH (SAHMSA 2014) revealed that the rate of current illicit drug (including marijuana) use was higher for people over 18-years-old who were unemployed (about 18%) than for those who were employed part time (about 14%) and for those who were employed full time (about 9%). Interestingly, those considered officially unemployed but who were engaged in other activities (such as students, persons keeping house or caring for children fulltime, retired or disabled persons, or people not in the labor force) had the least rate of self-reported illicit drug use.

Peer Influences

One of the most significant factors in young adult experimentation and initiation of marijuana use is the influence of their friends and peers. Haug et al., (2014) carried out an analysis of the Cohort Study on Substance Use Risk Factors (C-SURF) and discovered that peer pressure, among other factors, was directly associated with the decision to use or not to use marijuana. Also, the results of a four-year prospective study of risk factors for cannabis use and progression to abuse and dependence among adolescents and young adults showed that peer group pressure played an important role in experimentation with cannabis and progression to marijuana abuse disorders (von Sydow et al., 2002). Other studies (Kohn et al., 2004; Rumpold et al., 2006) have also confirmed the role of peers in the initiation and misuse of marijuana and other psychoactive substances.

Adverse Family Situations

Parents' marital disharmony, family history of drug abuse, parental antisocial behavior, poor communication, poor sibling and mother-child relationships and other adverse family situations have been shown to influence young adults to resort to the use of marijuana and other psychoactive substances. For instance, in the study by Haug et al., (2014), parental divorce was found to be one of the predictors of young adult marijuana initiation and misuse. Further a study carried out on 1760 respondents aged 18-23 years by Barrett et al., (2012) showed that respondents from single-parent families were significantly more likely to have a substance abuse disorder than those from families where both parents were present, even after controlling for race and gender. Murray et al., (2012) carried out a systematic review of the evidence on the association between parental incarceration and children's later antisocial behavior, drug use and other problems. They found that parental incarceration was associated with a high risk of young adult problematic behavior including the misuse and abuse of psychoactive substances such as marijuana. Other studies (Kohn et al., 2004; Velleman et al., 2005) have also emphasized the role of the family in determining the rates of initiation of and dependence on marijuana and other psychoactive substances among young adults.

Effects of Legalization and Regulation on Marijuana Use

Considered as the most widely used illicit drug worldwide, many authorities and governments have considered different forms of policies and reform options to assist them in addressing the use or misuse of marijuana. Currently, most of these governments, and authorities are faced with three policy options in dealing with marijuana use, namely: prohibition, decriminalization and legalization, with prohibition being the most prevalent option used worldwide (Room and Reuter 2012). In the United States, a perceived indicator of mass approval of marijuana use is the implementation of state marijuana laws. The authorization of physician-prescribed marijuana use for medical purposes in an effort to alleviate a myriad of symptoms for various illnesses is the desired purpose of these state laws. As a result of the substantial relationship that generally exists between public opinion and policy decisions, medical marijuana laws can be used to represent state-level norms on marijuana use (Burstein 2003; Burstein 2006; Brooks 2006; Nielsen 2010). According to Lipperman-Kreda and Grube (2009) and Lipperman-Kreda et al., (2010), policy and enforcement efforts are direct consequences of the various community norms with regards to substance use (e.g., drinking and cigarette smoking).

As early as 1996, in California, voters sanctioned what was known as the Compassionate Use Act. The Act dealt primarily with removing criminal penalties for use, possession, and cultivation of medical marijuana. This act made provision for doctors to prescribe marijuana to their patients for symptomatic relief of cancer, anorexia, AIDS, chronic pain, spasticity, glaucoma, arthritis, migraine, and other illnesses. Patients also had the priority of designating a caregiver that would be able to grow marijuana on their behalf. It is worth noting that the International Drug Control Convention is the body that governs marijuana globally. A great majority of the world's nations have implemented, and correspondingly signed into national prohibition, laws encompassing both marijuana use and production/supply. Recreational marijuana use and dissemination has only just been officially legalized under certain limitations by public referenda in two US states (Colorado and Washington).

The recent decriminalization and legalization of marijuana in certain states has led to increases in incidence and prevalence of marijuana use among young adults. Schuermeyer et al., (2014) analyzed the National Survey on Drug Use and Health (NSDUH) to test for changes in marijuana attitudes and marijuana-use-related outcomes in Colorado (a medical marijuana legal state) from 2003 to 2011. They compared the patterns of use before (2006-2008) to patterns during (2009-11) the legalization process. They also compared the rates of use between Colorado and other states where marijuana is not legal. The findings of the study indicated that, by 2010 to 2011, past-year marijuana abuse or dependence had increased in prevalence among young adults (18-25 years) in Colorado compared to states where marijuana was still illegal. The study also showed that legalization and commercialization had led to reduced perceived risk of marijuana use.

A similar study was carried out by Miech et al., (2015) in California. In this study, the trends in use of marijuana before legalization in the state in 2010 was compared to trends afterwards. The study showed that 12th graders (17-18 year olds) became 25% more likely to have used marijuana in the past 30 days and about 60% more likely to expect to be using marijuana five years in the future. Also, Cerda et al., (2012) also made similar discoveries when they analyzed the National Epidemiologic Survey on Alcohol and Related Conditions (NESARC). They found that adults (over 18 years old) who are residents of states with medical marijuana laws were more likely to use marijuana than similar populations in states without such laws.

HEALTH MESSAGES

Just like many other drugs, both legal and illegal, marijuana has beneficial and adverse effects. However, as a psychoactive substance, marijuana possesses the added potential for inducing addiction in users, leading to abuse and dependence. Thus, despite the known and purported benefits of marijuana, its non-medical (recreational) use should be discouraged because of the adverse health effects and the risk of addiction. Essentially, it should be used when the benefits to the individual outweigh the risks. More importantly, vulnerable and high risk groups such as children, adolescents and young adults need to be adequately educated and protected by regulations on marijuana marketing, purchase and use. Education of young people about marijuana should be focused on emphasizing that, even though some components of the marijuana plant have been found to be useful medically when isolated and purified, smoking marijuana is very dangerous to health. The current health messages by the Office of National Drug Control Policy (ONDCP), the National Criminal Justice Reference Service (NCJRS) and National Institute on Drug Abuse (NIDA) have been centered on deconstructing popular myths surrounding the use of marijuana (NCJRS nd; NIDA 2015b; ONDCP nd). Some of these myths and the evidence that debunks them are discussed below.

Myth 1: Marijuana is Harmless

Due to the discovery of medical uses of certain cannabinoids, many young people have been misled to think that marijuana is entirely harmless. To deconstruct this myth, it is important to emphasize that it is well known that marijuana use can lead to cognitive impairment, mental health problems, traffic accidents, and other problems related to abuse or dependence. Furthermore, smoked marijuana can cause lung damage and contains several chemicals which are known to be dangerous to health (NCJRS nd; NIDA 2015b; ONDCP nd).

Myth 2: Marijuana Is Not Addictive

This is a popular misconception among young people because of the high rate of experimentation with marijuana. Some young people try the substance and do not continue to use it afterwards, leading to the myth that it is not addictive. Indeed marijuana addiction is characterized by behaviors that fulfil the criteria for drug abuse and dependence (NCJRS nd; NIDA 2015b; ONDCP nd).

Myth 3: Marijuana Is Less Dangerous to Health Than Tobacco

Marijuana is currently being touted by some groups as a natural herb devoid of harmful chemicals present in tobacco. In reality, smoked marijuana contains many of the harmful, cancer-causing chemicals present in tobacco smoke. People who smoke marijuana have been found to develop the same breathing problems as people who use tobacco, and are at similar or even more risk of developing chronic lung and systemic diseases (NCJRS nd; NIDA 2015b; ONDCP nd).

Myth 4: Marijuana Calms People's Moods

While the mind-altering properties of marijuana are well known, smoking marijuana has not been known to calm people's moods. In fact, the euphoria and ecstasy associated with THC have been shown to reduce the natural inhibition that people have towards anti-social behavior. Marijuana use has therefore been associated with aggressive behavior, including attacking people, stealing, destroying property, and other criminal offenses (NCJRS nd; NIDA 2015b; ONDCP nd).

Myth 5: Marijuana Can Be Smoked to Treat Cancer and Other Diseases

While marijuana contains certain cannabinoids that can be extracted or synthesized and have proven useful for medicinal purposes, smoking marijuana has not been shown to provide these benefits and has actually been shown to do more harm than good. Even FDA-approved drugs containing marijuana-derived cannabinoids should be used with caution due to their adverse effects and, as with other drugs, should be used only when the benefits outweigh the risks (NCJRS nd; NIDA 2015b; ONDCP nd).

Similarly, the Substance Abuse and Mental Health Services (SAMHS) office of Maine Department of Health and Human Services (MDHHS) published a list of 5 key prevention messages regarding marijuana (MDHHS, 2014). Although these messages were directed at teens, the information is true for young adults as well. The 5 key prevention messages against recreational use of marijuana are:

1. *The impairment message:* the use of marijuana can hamper good judgement and self-control, leading to bad decisions and risky behavior.
2. *The health message:* the use of marijuana can cause damage to the brain, lungs and other parts of the body.
3. *The future/success message:* the use of marijuana can lead to attention and memory problems and has been linked to lower academic performance and reduced job prospects.
4. *The addiction message:* the use of marijuana can lead to addiction, which in turn leads to other health and safety problems.
5. *The harm perception message:* marijuana is not harmless, and the type currently produced for smoking is much more potent than before and therefore can cause even more harm.

Interventions to Reduce Marijuana Use among College Students

The college setting is a high-risk context for marijuana use. In fact, exaggerated perceptions of marijuana use among college students, may predispose them to think that they should join the crowd and thus reduce their previous attitudes and behaviors related to abstaining from marijuana use. Elliott and Carey (2012) evaluated the impact of an intervention to help college students who were abstainers to not begin using or to not try marijuana. The intervention that was examined was the Marijuana eCHECK UP TO GO (e-TOKE) for Universities and Colleges (San Diego State University Research Foundation 2015). This intervention was designed to correct young adults' misperceptions about others use of marijuana as well as to provide key prevention messages. Elliott and Carey (2012) examined the views of over 240 college students, most of whom were sophomores or juniors, who participated in the intervention. There was an intervention and a comparison group and results indicated that the e-TOKE intervention was successful in reducing misperceptions of marijuana use for those who participated in the intervention group. Students who viewed the web-based program also reported lower levels of disapproval from others for their decision to abstain from marijuana use. Consequently, Elliott and Carey concluded that this internet program was a successful prevention program, and that further research should be conducted to determine if the prevention program had the same positive outcomes over longer periods of time.

Stoddard et al., (2012) also examined the impact of online messages and information from peers on use of marijuana and alcohol for college students. These researchers reviewed the impact of virtual networks on college students' use of alcohol and marijuana. They used a survey to assess 3,448 college students' report of their own substance use. Results indicated that online peer support to avoid substance use had the potential to deter alcohol use for college students. The same relationship was not found for marijuana use. In terms of marijuana use, students who reported that they would regret substance use were less likely to report that they were using marijuana. Student report could have been influenced by the fact that marijuana use was illegal. The authors also pointed out that students may also have been aware that employers view online information and this could have affected their responses about marijuana use. The authors still concluded that online peer support to deter substance use could be helpful for college students, especially is pictures were used with lower levels of writing to provide prevention messages. In the future it will be important to continue to examine the impact of online support to deter substance use, as many students access the internet on even an hourly basis and it is a chief source of information for them.

In another web-based study, Lee et al., (2010) randomly assigned students who used marijuana and were transitioning from high school to college to receive web-based feedback about marijuana use or to participate in control conditions. One hundred and seventy-one students participated in the intervention and 170 were in the control groups. Those participating in the intervention received feedback about the pros and cons of their marijuana use, social and behavioral advantages of stopping marijuana use, negative consequences of marijuana use, and norms for using marijuana. This intervention did not yield effective results, and most of the high school students increased their use of marijuana during their transition to college. These researchers concluded that their intervention was not effective in reaching first-year college students, but might be more effective with older students who had a longer history of marijuana use. However, further research would be needed to determine if this were the case. It may be that a personal approach, were students talk to peers or trained counselors may be effective in reducing high school students' marijuana use in their transition from high school to college.

The personalized approach was effective in another study. For this study, Lee and her colleagues (2013) conducted an intervention to reduce marijuana use among college students. They identified 212 college students who reported using marijuana at least five times in the past month. Lee et al., randomly assigned students to participate in an intervention or to be in a control group. The intervention lasted an hour and was individualized for participants' needs. However, there were common ideas addressed with students including ideas about the patterns and consequences of marijuana use, ideas for reducing or stopping use, costs and benefits of stopping marijuana use, how much marijuana cost the student, and information about use of other substances. Students participating in the intervention reported lower marijuana use and fewer negative consequences related to use compared to students who were in the control group at a 3-month follow up assessment.

CONCLUSION

This chapter has presented information on the current issues with marijuana use and the effects of its legalization on college-age young adults. The research we have reviewed shows that college-age young adults (18-25 years) are at great risk of marijuana misuse and the subsequent negative consequences. These consequences include acute adverse reactions, addiction/dependence, and higher risk of vehicular accidents while under its influence. Research also shows that marijuana, like any drug, has both useful and adverse effects which depend on how it is used. Active components (cannabinoids) of the marijuana plant, when extracted or synthesized, can be used for a growing range of medicinal purposes. Conversely, the smoked raw form carries the risk of more adverse effects than benefits and much of the current clamor for the legalization of marijuana does not distinguish between the two extremes. Furthermore, the research we have reviewed shows that marijuana use has increased among college-age young adults in states where legalization has occurred, and perception of risks of marijuana misuse has decreased among the same population in these states.

With the background of the ongoing legalization and decriminalization efforts, we advise a discretionary approach – one that acknowledges the established and potential benefits of marijuana extracts for medicinal use while bearing in mind its possible adverse effects. Much more research is needed to understand and appreciate the full extent of marijuana's medicinal uses and undesirable effects, and legislation should encourage this research until the right place of marijuana in medicine and society is better understood. Meanwhile, medical marijuana should be subject to similar precautionary measures as opioids and other prescription medication with high risks of abuse, while recreational use should be discouraged. It is also important that marijuana laws should protect vulnerable populations that are known to be at high risk for misuse, abuse and addiction.

There are several myths that surround the use of marijuana and it is important to clarify these misconceptions based on existing evidence. Despite the contrary opinions of some groups, marijuana use is not harmless, can lead to addiction, can cause memory problems which can lead to lower academic performance, and can result in loss of inhibition and consequent anti-social behavior. Thus health messages that address these myths should be communicated in diverse and inclusive ways, through the media, advocacy efforts and interpersonal communication. Interventions to deliver accurate information, debunk myths and offer help have been shown to be effective when personalized and organized in college settings. Also, online interventions are gaining more popularity as the use of the internet expands exponentially among young people. Through these and other means, the perception of marijuana as a drug with both beneficial and adverse effects should be maintained, especially among groups that are most at risk for misuse, in order to protect the health of young people.

References

Abdullaev, Yalchin, Michael I. Posner, Ray Nunnally, and Thomas J. Dishion. 2010. "Functional MRI evidence for inefficient attentional control in adolescent chronic cannabis abuse." *Behavioural Brain Research* 215:45-57. Accessed October 4, 2015. doi: 10.1016/j.bbr.2010.06.023.

Aldington, Sarah, Matire Harwood, Brian Cox, Mark Weatherall, Lutz Beckert, Anna Hansell, Alison Pritchard, Geoffrey Robinson, and Richard Beasley. 2008. "Cannabis use and risk of lung cancer: a case–control study." *European Respiratory Journal* 31:280-286. Accessed November 2, 2015. doi: 10.1183/09031936.00065707.

Arria, Amelia M., Kimberly M. Caldeira, Brittany A. Bugbee, Kathryn B. Vincent, and Kevin E. O'Grady. 2015. "The academic consequences of marijuana use during college." *Psychology of Addictive Behaviors* 29:564. Accessed October 2, 2015. doi: 10.1037/adb0000108.

Barrett, Anne E., and R. Jay Turner. 2006. "Family structure and substance use problems in adolescence and early adulthood: examining explanations for the relationship." *Addiction* 101:109-120. Accessed October 19, 2015. doi: 10.1111/j.1360-0443.2005.01296.x.

Becker, Benjamin, Daniel Wagner, Euphrosyne Gouzoulis-Mayfrank, Elmar Spuentrup, and Jörg Daumann. 2010. "The impact of early-onset cannabis use on functional brain correlates of working memory." *Progress in Neuro-Psychopharmacology and Biological Psychiatry* 34:837-845. Accessed October 19, 2015. doi: 10.1016/j.pnpbp.2010.03.032.

Berg, Carla J., Erin Stratton, Gillian L. Schauer, Michael Lewis, Yanwen Wang, Michael Windle, and Michelle Kegler. 2015. "Perceived harm, addictiveness, and social acceptability of tobacco products and marijuana among young adults: marijuana, hookah, and electronic cigarettes win." *Substance Use & Misuse* 50:79-89. Accessed October 18, 2015. doi: 10.3109/10826084.2014.958857.

Berthiller, Julien, Kurt Straif, Mathieu Boniol, Nicolas Voirin, Veronique Benhaïm-Luzon, Wided Ben Ayoub, Iman Dari, Slimane Laouamri, Mokhtar Hamdi-Cherif, Mohamed Bartal, Fahrat B. Ayed, and Annie J. Sasco. 2008. "Cannabis smoking and risk of lung cancer in men: a pooled analysis of three studies in Maghreb." *Journal of Thoracic Oncology* 3:1398-1403. Accessed October 18, 2015. doi: 10.1097/JTO.0b013e 31818ddcde.

Bisogno, Tiziana, Dominique Melck, MYu Bobrov, N. Gretskaya, V. Bezuglov, Luciano De Petrocellis, and Vincenzo Di Marzo. 2000. "N-acyl-dopamines: novel synthetic CB1 cannabinoid-receptor ligands and inhibitors of anandamide inactivation with cannabimimetic activity in vitro and in vivo." *Biochemical Journal* 351:817-824. Accessed October 24, 2015. doi: 10.1042/0264-6021:3510817.

Bonn-Miller, Marcel O., Michael J. Zvolensky, and Amit Bernstein. 2007. "Marijuana use motives: Concurrent relations to frequency of past 30-day use and anxiety sensitivity among young adult marijuana smokers." *Addictive Behaviors* 32:49-62. Accessed October 21, 2015. doi: 10.1016/j.addbeh.2006.03.018.

Brooks, Clem. 2006. "Voters, satisficing, and policymaking: recent directions in the study of electoral politics." *Annual Review of Sociology* 191-211. Accessed October 3, 2015. doi: 10.1146/annurev.soc.32.061604.1231 42.

Budney, Alan J. 2006. "Are specific dependence criteria necessary for different substances: how can research on cannabis inform this issue?" *Addiction* 101:125-133. Accessed October 2, 2015. doi: 10.1111/j.1360-0443.2006.01582.x.

Budney, Alan J., Roger Roffman, Robert S. Stephens, and Denise Walker. 2007. "Marijuana dependence and its treatment." *Addiction Science & Clinical practice* 4:4. Accessed October 2, 2015. doi: 10.1151/ASCP07414.

Budney, Alan J., and Catherine Stanger. 2012. "Cannabis use and misuse." In *IACAPRP e-textbook of child and adolescent mental health*, edited by Joseph M. Rey, 1-28. Geneva: International Association for Child and Adolescent Psychiatry and Allied Professions. Accessed October 24, 2015. http://iacapap.org/wp-content/uploads/G.2-CANNABIS-072012.pdf.

Burstein, Paul. 2003. "The impact of public opinion on public policy: A review and an agenda." *Political Research Quarterly* 56:29-40. Accessed October 24, 2015. doi: 10.1177/106591290305600103.

Burstein, Paul. 2006. "Why estimates of the impact of public opinion on public policy are too high: Empirical and theoretical implications." *Social Forces* 84:2273-2289. Accessed October 22, 2015. doi: 10.1353/sof.2006.0083.

California Department of Public Health (CDPH). 2015. "Proposition 215." Accessed October 24, 2015. https://www.cdph.ca.gov/programs/MMP/Pages/CompassionateUseact.aspx.

Callaghan, Russell C., Peter Allebeck, and Anna Sidorchuk. 2013. "Marijuana use and risk of lung cancer: a 40-year cohort study." *Cancer Causes & Control* 24:1811-1820. Accessed October 24, 2015. doi: 10.1007/s10552-013-0259-0.

Caspi, Avshalom, Terrie E. Moffitt, Mary Cannon, Joseph McClay, Robin Murray, HonaLee Harrington, Alan Taylor, Louise Arseneault, Ben Williams, Antony Braithwaite, Richie Poulton, and Ian W. Craig. 2005. "Moderation of the effect of adolescent-onset cannabis use on adult psychosis by a functional polymorphism in the catechol-O-methyltransferase gene: longitudinal evidence of a gene X environment interaction." *Biological Psychiatry* 57:1117-1127. Accessed October 12, 2015. doi: 10.1016/j.biopsych.2005.01.026.

Center for Substance Abuse Treatment. 2004. "Appendix C DSM-IV-TR material: criteria for substance dependence" In *Clinical guidelines for the use of buprenorphine in the treatment of opioid addiction*, edited by

Substance Abuse and Mental Health Services Administration (US). Rockville: Substance Abuse and Mental Health Services Administration (US). Accessed October 24, 2015. http://www.ncbi.nlm.nih.gov/books/NBK64247/.

Cerdá, Magdalena, Melanie Wall, Katherine M. Keyes, Sandro Galea, and Deborah Hasin. 2012. "Medical marijuana laws in 50 states: investigating the relationship between state legalization of medical marijuana and marijuana use, abuse and dependence." *Drug and Alcohol Dependence* 120:22-27. Accessed October 24, 2015. doi: 10.1016/j.drugalcdep.2011.06.011.

Chen, Chuan-Yu, Carla L. Storr, and James C. Anthony. 2009. "Early-onset drug use and risk for drug dependence problems." *Addictive Behaviors* 34:319-322. Accessed October 15, 2015. doi: 10.1016/j.addbeh.2008.10.021.

Cohn, Amy, Andrea Villanti, Amanda Richardson, Jessica M. Rath, Valerie Williams, Cassandra Stanton, and Robin Mermelstein. 2015. "The association between alcohol, marijuana use, and new and emerging tobacco products in a young adult population." *Addictive Behaviors* 48:79-88. Accessed October 15, 2015. doi: 10.1016/j.addbeh.2015.02.005.

Copeland, Jan, Wendy Swift, Roger Roffman, and Robert Stephens. 2001. "A randomized controlled trial of brief cognitive–behavioral interventions for cannabis use disorder." *Journal of Substance Abuse Treatment* 21:55-64. Accessed October 15, 2015. doi: 10.1016/S0740-5472(01)00179-9.

Daling, Janet R., David R. Doody, Xiaofei Sun, Britton L. Trabert, Noel S. Weiss, Chu Chen, Mary L. Biggs, Jacqueline R. Starr, Sudhansu K. Dey, and Stephen M. Schwartz. 2009. "Association of marijuana use and the incidence of testicular germ cell tumors." *Cancer* 115: 1215-1223. Accessed October 24, 2015. doi: 10.1002/cncr.24159.

Di Forti, Marta, Hannah Sallis, Fabio Allegri, Antonella Trotta, Laura Ferraro, Simona A. Stilo, Arianna Marconi, Caterina La Cascia, Tiago Reis Marques, Carmine Pariante, Paola Dazzan, Valeria Mondelli, Alessandra Paparelli, Anna Kolliakou, Diana Prata, Fiona Gaughran, Anthony S. David, Craig Morgan, Daniel Stahl, Mizanur Khondoker, James H. MacCabe, and Robin M. Murray. 2014. "Daily use, especially of high-potency cannabis, drives the earlier onset of psychosis in cannabis users." *Schizophrenia Bulletin* 40:1509-1517. Accessed October 24, 2015. doi: 10.1093/schbul/sbt181.

Elliott, Jennifer C., and Kate B. Carey. 2012. "Correcting exaggerated marijuana use norms among college abstainers: A preliminary test of a preventive intervention." *Journal of Studies on Alcohol and Drugs* 73:976-980. Accessed October 12, 2015. doi: 10.15288/jsad.2012.73.976.

Gable, Robert S. 2004. "Comparison of acute lethal toxicity of commonly abused psychoactive substances." *Addiction* 99:686-696. Accessed October 18, 2015. https://www.thevespiary.org/rhodium/Rhodium/pdf/psychoactives.acute.lethal.toxicity.pdf.

Gerberich, Susan Goodwin, Stephen Sidney, Barbara L. Braun, Irene S. Tekawa, Kimberly K. Tolan, and Charles P. Quesenberry. 2003. "Marijuana use and injury events resulting in hospitalization." *Annals of Epidemiology* 13: 230-237. Accessed October 24, 2015. doi: 10.1016/S1047-2797(02)00411-8.

Gogtay, Nitin, Jay N. Giedd, Leslie Lusk, Kiralee M. Hayashi, Deanna Greenstein, A. Catherine Vaituzis, Tom F. Nugent, David H. Herman, Liv S. Clasen, Arthur W. Toga, Judith L. Rapoport, and Paul M. Thompson. 2004. "Dynamic mapping of human cortical development during childhood through early adulthood." Proceedings of the National Academy of Sciences of the United States of America 101:8174-8179. Accessed October 24, 2015. doi: 10.1073/pnas.0402680101.

Goldenberg, David, Juna Lee, Wayne M. Koch, Michael M. Kim, Barry Trink, David Sidransky, and Chul-So Moon. 2004. "Habitual risk factors for head and neck cancer." *Otolaryngology-Head and Neck Surgery* 131:986-993. Accessed October 13, 2015. doi:10.1016/j.otohns.2004.02.035.

Grotenhermen, Franjo, Gero Leson, Günter Berghaus, Olaf H. Drummer, Hans-Peter Krüger, Marie Longo, Herbert Moskowitz, Bud Perrine, Johannes G. Ramaekers, Alison Smiley, and Rob Tunbridge. 2007. "Developing limits for driving under cannabis." *Addiction* 102:1910-1917. Accessed October 13, 2015. doi: 10.1111/j.1360-0443.2007.02009.x.

Grotenhermen, Franjo, and Kirsten Müller-Vahl. 2012. "The therapeutic potential of cannabis and cannabinoids." *Deutsches Ärzteblatt International* 109:495. Accessed October 13, 2015. doi: 10.3238/arztebl.2012.0495.

Guindon, Josée, André De Léan, and Pierre Beaulieu. 2006. "Local interactions between anandamide, an endocannabinoid, and ibuprofen, a nonsteroidal anti-inflammatory drug, in acute and inflammatory pain." *Pain* 121:85-93. Accessed October 2, 2015. doi: 10.1016/j.pain.2005.12.007.

Hall, Wayne. 2009. "The adverse health effects of cannabis use: What are they, and what are their implications for policy?" *International Journal of drug policy* 20:458-466. Accessed October 2, 2015. doi: 10.1016/j.drugpo. 2009.02.013.

Hall, Wayne, and Louisa Degenhardt. 2007. "Prevalence and correlates of cannabis use in developed and developing countries." *Current Opinion in Psychiatry* 20:393-397. Accessed October 5, 2015. doi: 10.1097/YCO. 0b013e32812144cc.

Hall, Wayne, and Louisa Degenhardt. 2009. "Adverse health effects of non-medical cannabis use." *The Lancet* 374:1383-1391. Accessed October 12, 2015. doi: 10.1016/S0140-6736 (09)61037-0.

Hanson, Margaret D., and Edith Chen. 2007. "Socioeconomic status and health behaviors in adolescence: a review of the literature." *Journal of Behavioral Medicine* 30:263-285. Accessed October 5, 2015. doi: 10.1007/s10865-007-9098-3.

Hashibe, Mia, Daniel E. Ford, and Zuo-Feng Zhang. 2002. "Marijuana smoking and head and neck cancer." *Journal of Clinical Pharmacology* 42:103-107. Accessed October 8, 2015. doi: 10.1002/j.1552-4604.2002. tb06010.x.

Haug, Severin, Carla López Núñez, Julia Becker, Gerhard Gmel, and Michael P. Schaub. 2014. "Predictors of onset of cannabis and other drug use in male young adults: results from a longitudinal study." *BMC Public Health* 14:1202. Accessed October 8, 2015. doi: 10.1186/1471-2458-14-1202.

Hoch, Eva, Udo Bonnet, Rainer Thomasius, Florian Ganzer, Ursula Havemann-Reinecke, and Ulrich W. Preuss. 2015. "Risks associated with the non-medicinal use of cannabis." *Deutsches Ärzteblatt International* 112:271. Accessed October 28, 2015. doi: 10.3238/arztebl.2015.0271.

Jager, Gerry, Robert I. Block, Maartje Luijten, and Nick F. Ramsey. 2010. "Cannabis use and memory brain function in adolescent boys: A cross-sectional multicenter functional magnetic resonance imaging study." *Journal of the American Academy of Child & Adolescent Psychiatry* 49:561-572. Accessed October 12, 2015. doi: 10.1016/j.jaac.2010.02.001.

Kalant, Harold. 2004. "Adverse effects of cannabis on health: an update of the literature since 1996." *Progress in Neuro-psychopharmacology and Biological Psychiatry* 28:849-863. Accessed October 9, 2015. doi: 10.1016/j.drugpo.2009.02.013.

Kohn, Laurence, France Kittel, and Danielle Piette. 2004. "Peer, family integration and other determinants of cannabis use among teenagers." *International Journal of Adolescent Medicine and health* 16:359-370. Accessed October 13, 2015. doi: 10.1515/IJAMH.2004.16.4.359.

Lacson, John Charles A., Joshua D. Carroll, Ellenie Tuazon, Esteban J. Castelao, Leslie Bernstein, and Victoria K. Cortessis. 2012. "Population-based case-control study of recreational drug use and testis cancer risk confirms an association between marijuana use and nonseminoma risk." *Cancer* 118:5374-5383. Accessed October 23, 2015. doi: 10.1002/cncr. 27554.

Lee, Christine M., Jason R. Kilmer, Clayton Neighbors, David C. Atkins, Cheng Zheng, Denise D. Walker, and Mary E. Larimer. 2013. "Indicated prevention for college student marijuana use: a randomized controlled trial." *Journal of Consulting and Clinical Psychology* 81:702. Accessed October 24, 2015. doi: 10.1037/a0033285.

Lee, Christine M., Clayton Neighbors, Jason R. Kilmer, and Mary E. Larimer. 2010. "A brief, web-based personalized feedback selective intervention for college student marijuana use: a randomized clinical trial." *Psychology of Addictive Behaviors* 24:265. Accessed October 23, 2015. doi: 10.1037/a0018859.

Lipperman-Kreda, Sharon, and Joel W. Grube. 2009. "Students' perception of community disapproval, perceived enforcement of school antismoking policies, personal beliefs, and their cigarette smoking behaviors: results from a structural equation modeling analysis." *Nicotine & Tobacco Research* 11:531-539. Accessed October 8, 2015. doi: 10.1093/ntr/ntp033.

Lipperman-Kreda, Sharon, Joel W. Grube, and Mallie J. Paschall. 2010."Community norms, enforcement of minimum legal drinking age laws, personal beliefs and underage drinking: an explanatory model." *Journal of Community Health* 35:249-257. Accessed October 9, 2015. doi: 10.1007/s10900-010-9229-6.

Lopez-Quintero, Catalina, José Pérez de los Cobos, Deborah S. Hasin, Mayumi Okuda, Shuai Wang, Bridget F. Grant, and Carlos Blanco. 2010. "Probability and predictors of transition from first use to dependence on nicotine, alcohol, cannabis, and cocaine: Results of the National Epidemiologic Survey on Alcohol and Related Conditions (NESARC)." *Drug and Alcohol Dependence* 115:120-130. Accessed October 14, 2015. doi: 10.1016/j.drugalcdep.2010.11.004.

Maine Department of Health and Human Services (MDHHS). 2014. "Maine SAMHS 5 key prevention messages regarding marijuana." Accessed October 12, 2015. http://www.maine.gov/dhhs/samhs/osa/prevention/pdfs/updated%20SAMHS%20Key%20Prev%20MJ%20Messages.pdf.

Manzanares, J., M. D. Julian, and A. Carrascosa. 2015. "Role of the cannabinoid system in pain control and therapeutic implications for the management of acute and chronic pain episodes." *Current Neuropharmacology* 4:239. Accessed October 9, 2015. doi: 10.2174/157015906778019527.

Mechoulam, Raphael, and Lumír Hanuš. 2000. "A historical overview of chemical research on cannabinoids." *Chemistry and Physics of Lipids* 108:1-13. Accessed October 2, 2015. doi: 10.1016/S0009-3084(00)00184-5.

Mechoulam, Raphael, and Linda A. Parker. 2013. "The endocannabinoid system and the brain." *Annual Review of Psychology* 64:21-47. Accessed October 25, 2015. doi: 10.1146/annurev-psych-113011-143739.

Menghrajani, Pareesa, Karen Klaue, Françoise Dubois-Arber, and P-A. Michaud. 2005. "Swiss adolescents' and adults' perceptions of cannabis use: A qualitative study." *Health Education Research* 20:476-484. Accessed October 24, 2015. doi: 10.1093/her/cyh003.

Mehra, Reena, Brent A. Moore, Kristina Crothers, Jeanette Tetrault, and David A. Fiellin. 2006. "The association between marijuana smoking and lung cancer: a systematic review." *Archives of Internal Medicine* 166:1359-1367. Accessed November 2, 2015. doi: 10.1001/archinte.166.13.1359.

Miech, Richard A., Lloyd Johnston, Patrick M. O'Malley, Jerald G. Bachman, John Schulenberg, and Megan E. Patrick. 2015. "Trends in use of marijuana and attitudes toward marijuana among youth before and after decriminalization: The case of California 2007–2013." *International Journal of Drug Policy* 26:336-344. Accessed October 25, 2015. doi: 10.1016/j.drugpo.2015.01.009.

Murray, Joseph, David P. Farrington, and Ivana Sekol. 2012 "Children's antisocial behavior, mental health, drug use, and educational performance after parental incarceration: a systematic review and meta-analysis." *Psychological Bulletin* 138:175. Accessed October 29, 2015. doi: 10.1037/a0026407.

National Criminal Justice Reference Service (NCJRS). nd. "Marijuana myths and facts: The truth behind 10 popular misconceptions." Accessed October 30, 2015. https://www.ncjrs.gov/ondcppubs/publications/pdf/marijuana_myths_facts.pdf.

National Institute on Drug Abuse (NIDA). 2015a. "DrugFacts: Is marijuana medicine?" Accessed October 29, 2015. https://www.drugabuse.gov/publications/drugfacts/marijuana-medicine.

National Institute on Drug Abuse (NIDA). 2015b. "DrugFacts: Marijuana." Accessed October 29, 2015. https://www.drugabuse.gov/publications/drugfacts/marijuana.

Nielsen, Amie L. 2010. "Americans' Attitudes toward Drug-Related Issues from 1975–2006: The Roles of Period and Cohort Effects." *Journal of Drug Issues* 40:461-493. Accessed October 15, 2015. doi: 10.1177/002204261004000209.

Office of National Drug Control Policy. nd. "Answers to Frequently Asked Questions about Marijuana." Accessed October 8, 2015. https://www.whitehouse.gov/ondcp/frequently-asked-questions-and-facts-about-marijuana.

Pacher, Pál, Sándor Bátkai, and George Kunos. 2006. "The endocannabinoid system as an emerging target of pharmacotherapy." *Pharmacological Reviews* 58:389-462. Accessed October 12, 2015. doi: 10.1124/pr.58.3.2.

Patton, George C., Carolyn Coffey, John B. Carlin, Louisa Degenhardt, Michael Lynskey, and Wayne Hall. 2002. "Cannabis use and mental health in young people: cohort study." *BMJ* 325:1195-1198. Accessed October 20, 2015. doi: 10.1136/bmj.325.7374.1195.

Pazos, María Ruth, Estefanía Núñez, Cristina Benito, Rosa María Tolón, and Julián Romero. 2005. "Functional neuroanatomy of the endocannabinoid system." *Pharmacology Biochemistry and Behavior* 81:239-247. Accessed October 24, 2015. doi: 10.1016/j.pbb.2005.01.030.

Pujazon-Zazik, Melissa, and M. Jane Park. 2009. "Marijuana: use among young males and health outcomes." *American Journal of Men's Health* 3:265-274. Accessed October 14, 2015. doi: 10.1177/1557988309340577.

Ramaekers, Johannes G., Günter Berghaus, Margriet van Laar, and Olaf H. Drummer. 2004. "Dose related risk of motor vehicle crashes after cannabis use." *Drug and Alcohol Dependence* 73:109-119. Accessed October 8, 2015. doi: 10.1016/j.drugalcdep.2003.10.008.

Redonnet, Bertrand, Aude Chollet, Eric Fombonne, Lucy Bowes, and Maria Melchior. 2012. "Tobacco, alcohol, cannabis and other illegal drug use among young adults: the socioeconomic context." *Drug and Alcohol Dependence* 121:231-239. Accessed October 22, 2015. doi: 10.1016/j.drugalcdep.2011.09.002.

Room, Robin, and Peter Reuter. 2012. "How well do international drug conventions protect public health?" *The Lancet* 379:84-91. Accessed October 24, 2015. doi: 10.1016/S0140-6736(11)61423-2.

Rumpold, Gerhard, Michael Klingseis, Kurt Dornauer, Martin Kopp, Stephan Doering, Stefan Höfer, Birgit Mumelter, and Gerhard Schüßler. 2006. "Psychotropic Substance Abuse Among Adolescents: A Structural Equation Model on Risk and Protective Factors." *Substance Use & Misuse*

41:1155-1169. Accessed October 24, 2015. doi: 10.1080/10826080600752136.

San Diego State University Research Foundation. 2015. "Marijuana eCHECKUP TO GO (e-TOKE) for Universities & Colleges." Accessed October 20, 2015. http://www.echeckuptogo.com/usa/programs/coll_mj.php.

Schuermeyer, Joseph, Stacy Salomonsen-Sautel, Rumi Kato Price, Sundari Balan, Christian Thurstone, Sung-Joon Min, and Joseph T. Sakai. 2014. "Temporal trends in marijuana attitudes, availability and use in Colorado compared to non-medical marijuana states: 2003–11." *Drug and Alcohol Dependence* 140:145-155. Accessed October 21, 2015. doi: 10.1016/j.drugalcdep.2014.04.016.

Schweinsburg, Alecia Dager, Brian C. Schweinsburg, Krista Lisdahl Medina, Tim McQueeny, Sandra A. Brown, and Susan F. Tapert. 2010. "The influence of recency of use on fMRI response during spatial working memory in adolescent marijuana users." *Journal of Psychoactive Drugs* 42:401-412. Accessed October 14, 2015. doi: 10.1080/02791072.2010.10400703.

Shoemaker, Jennifer L., Michael B. Ruckle, Philip R. Mayeux, and Paul L. Prather. 2005. "Agonist-directed trafficking of response by endocannabinoids acting at CB2 receptors." *Journal of Pharmacology and Experimental Therapeutics* 315: 828-838. Accessed October 24, 2015. doi: 10.1124/jpet.105.089474. PMID 16081674.

Stephens, Robert S., Thomas F. Babor, Ronald Kadden, and Michael Miller. 2002. "The Marijuana Treatment Project: rationale, design and participant characteristics." *Addiction* 97:109-124. Accessed October 19, 2015. doi: 10.1046/j.1360-0443.97.s01.6.x.

Stoddard, Sarah A., Jose A. Bauermeister, Deborah Gordon-Messer, Michelle Johns, and Marc A. Zimmerman. "Permissive norms and young adults' alcohol and marijuana use: The role of online communities." *Journal of Studies on Alcohol and Drugs* 73: 968-975. Accessed October 24, 2015. doi: 10.15288/jsad.2012.73.968.

Substance Abuse and Mental Health Services Administration. 2014. *Results from the 2013 National Survey on Drug Use and Health: Summary of National Findings*. Rockville, MD: Substance Abuse and Mental Health Services Administration. Accessed October 28, 2015. http://www.samhsa.gov/data/sites/default/files/NSDUHresultsPDFWHTML2013/Web/NSDUHresults2013.pdf.

Trabert, Britton, Alice J. Sigurdson, Anne M. Sweeney, Sara S. Strom, and Katherine A. McGlynn. 2011. "Marijuana use and testicular germ cell tumors." *Cancer* 117: 848-853. October 22, 2015. doi: 10.1002/cncr.25499.

United Nations Office on Drugs and Crime (UNODC). 2015. "About UNDOC." Accessed October 22, 2015. https://www.unodc.org/unodc/en/about-unodc/index.html?ref=menutop.

Velleman, Richard DB, Lorna J. Templeton, and Alex G. Copello. 2005. "The role of the family in preventing and intervening with substance use and misuse: a comprehensive review of family interventions, with a focus on young people." *Drug and Alcohol Review* 24:93-109. Accessed October 28, 2015. doi: 10.1080/09595230500167478.

Voirin, Nicolas, Julien Berthiller, Véronique Benhaïm-Luzon, Mathieu Boniol, Kurt Straif, Wided Ben Ayoub, Fahrat Ben Ayed, and Annie J. Sasco. 2006. "Risk of lung cancer and past use of cannabis in Tunisia." *Journal of Thoracic Oncology* 1:577-579. Accessed October 28, 2015. http://journals.lww.com/jto/Fulltext/2006/07000/Risk_of_Lung_Cancer_and_Past_Use_of_Cannabis_in.13.

Von Sydow, Kirsten, Roselind Lieb, Hildegard Pfister, Michael Höfler, and Hans-Ulrich Wittchen. 2002. "What predicts incident use of cannabis and progression to abuse and dependence?: A 4-year prospective examination of risk factors in a community sample of adolescents and young adults." *Drug and Alcohol Dependence* 68:49-64. Accessed October 13, 2015. doi: 10.1016/S0376-8716(02)00102-3.

BIOGRAPHICAL SKETCH

Name: Laura Nabors, Ph.D.
Affiliation: Health Promotion and Education Program, University of Cincinnati
Date of Birth: 7/12/1963
Education: PhD

Address: Mail Location 0068, School of Human Services, University of Cincinnati, Cincinnati, Ohio 45221-0068

Research and Professional Experience: 20 years of experience as a researcher in health services

Professional Appointments: Associate Professor University of Cincinnati

Honors: Fellow American Psychological Association
Publications Last Three Years:

Nabors, L. & Iobst, E. A. (2012). Young adults' perceptions of dental procedures. *International Journal of Applied Science and Technology. 2*(2), 106-109.

Vaughn, L. M., Nabors, L., Pelley, T. J., Hampton, R. R., & Jacquez, F. (2012). Obesity screening in the pediatric emergency department. *Pediatric Emergency Care*, *28*(6), 548-552.

Brubaker, M. D., Nabors, L. A., Pangallo, J., & Shipley, H. (2012). Stigmatization of adolescents who use alcohol and marijuana: A counseling concern. *Ideas and Research You Can Use: VISTAS 2012*. http://www.counseling.org/resources/library/VISTAS/vistas12/2012_Vol_1_45-66/Article_64.pdf.

Nabors, L. A., Brubaker, M. D., Hoffman, S., Shipman, H., Pangallo, J., & Strong, A. (2012). Young adults' perceptions of an adolescent's use of marijuana and alcohol. *Journal of Drug Education, 42*(4), 413-424.

Vidourek, R. A., King, K. A., Bernard, A. L., Nabors, L. A., & Murnan, J. (2012). Teachers' perceived benefits and barriers to connecting students to school. *American Journal of Health Studies, 27*(3), 136-145.

Rosenzweig, K. J., & Nabors, L. (2013). Pain coping strategies for children with arthritis, in Rheumatology, BioMed Research International, vol. 2013, Article ID 741428, 3 pages. doi:10.1155/2013/741428.

Nabors, L. A., Kichler, J. C., Brassell, A., Thakkar, S., Bartz, J., Pangallo, J., Van Wassenhove, B., & Lundy, H. (2013). Factors related to caregiver state anxiety and coping with a child's chronic illness. *Families, Systems, and Health, 31*(2), 171-180.

Kichler, J. C., Kaugars, A. S., Marik, P., Nabors, L., & Alemzadeh, R. (Sept 9, 2013). Effectiveness of groups for adolescents with Type I Diabetes Mellitus and their Parents. *Families, Systems, and Health*, *31*(3), Sep 2013, 280-293.

Brubaker, M. D., Garrett, M. T., Amatea, E. A., Rivera, E. T. Miller, M. D., & Nabors, L. (2013). Barriers and supports to substance abuse service utilization among homeless adults. *Journal of Addictions and Offender* Counseling, *34*(2), 81-98.

Merianos, A. L., Nabors, L. A., King, K. A., & Vidourek, R. A. (2013). Perceptions of pain and resilience factors among male and female college students. *Journal of Behavioral Health*, *2*(4), 299-307. doi: 10.5455/jbh.20130918011022.

Amin, P., Levin, L., Smith, A., Davis, B., Nabors, L., & Bernstein, J. A. (2013). Asthma screening of inner city and urban elementary school-aged children. *Journal of Asthma*, *50*(10), 1049-1055.

Nabors, L., Bartz, J., Kichler, J., Sievers, R., Elkins, R., & Pangallo, J. (2013). Play as a mechanism of working through medical trauma for children with medical illnesses and their siblings. *Issues in Comprehensive Pediatric Nursing*, *36*(3), 212-224.

Nabors, L., Burbage, M., Pangallo, J., Bernard, A., Gardocki, S., Strong, A., Shelton, P., & Jones, D. (2013). Delivery and evaluation of a pilot obesity prevention project for urban Appalachian children. *Open Journal of Pediatrics, 3*, 300-305. http://dx.doi.org/10.4236/ojped.2013.34054 Published Online December 2013 (http://www.scirp.org/journal/ojped/).

Merianos, A. L., Nabors, L., Vidourek, R. A., & King, K. A. (2014). The Impact of Self-Esteem and Social Support on College Students' Mental Health. *American Journal of Health Studies, 28*(1), 27-34.

Nabors, L. A., Mason, M., & Bernstein, J. A., (2014, May). Asthma camps for children. *Journal of Asthma*, *51*(4), 339-340.

Veeneman, N., Nabors, L., & Rohan, J. M. (2014). Middle school-age children's acceptance of a child with a facial scar. *International Journal of Child and Adolescent Health*, *7*(3), 213-217.

Vidourek, R. A., King, K. A., Nabors, L. A., & Merianos, A. L. (2014). Students' benefits and barriers to mental health help-seeking. *Health Psychology and Behavioral Medicine, 2*(1), 1009-1022. DOI: 10.1080/21642850.2014.963586.

Vidourek, R. A., King, K. A., Nabors, L. A., Lynch, A. N., & Merianos, A. L. (2014). College students' perceived confidence in mental health help-seeking. *International Journal of Mental Health Promotion*, 16(2), 83-90.

Dia, C-L, Nabors, L. A., King, K. A., Vidourek, R. A., Chen, C-C, Hoang, N., & Mastro, K. G. (2014). Evaluation of an afterschool children's healthy eating and exercise program. *International Journal of Child Health and Nutrition, 3*(4), 156-162.

Nabors, L. A., Kichler, J. C., Burbage, M. L., Swoboda, C. M., & Andreone, T. L. (2014). Children's Learning and Goal-Setting at a Diabetes Camp. *Diabetes Spectrum*, *27*(4), 257-263.

Merianos, A. L., King, K. A., Vidourek, R. A., & Nabors, L. A. (2015). Recent alcohol use and binge drinking based on authoritative parenting among Hispanic youth nationwide. *Journal of Child and Family Studies, 24(7),* 1966-1976.

Dai, C-L, Nabors, L., Vidourek, R. A., King, K. A., and Chen, C. C. (2015). Letter to the Editor: Evaluation of an after-school yoga program. *International Journal of Yoga*, *8*, 1-2.

Nabors, L., Burbage, M., Woodson, K., & Swoboda, C. (2015). Implementation of an After-School Obesity Prevention Program: Helping young children toward improved health. *Issues in Comprehensive Pediatric Nursing, 38(1), 22-38.* doi:10.3109/01460862.2014.

Woodson, K. D., Thakkar, S., Burbage, M., Kichler, J., & Nabors, L. (2015). Children with chronic illnesses: Factors influencing family hardiness. *Issues in Comprehensive Pediatric Nursing*, *38*(1), 57-69. doi:10.3109/01460862.2014.988896.

Elkins, R., Nabors, L., King, K., & Vidourek, R. (2015). Factors influencing expectations of physical activity for adolescents residing in Appalachia. *American Journal of Health Education, 46*(1), 7-12.

Sanning, B., & Nabors, L. (January 15, 2015). Indicators of flourishing in anxious preschool-aged children. *International Journal of Mental Health Promotion*, (ahead-of-print), 1-9. DOI: 10.1080/14623730.2014.999455.

Burbage, M. L., Mason, M., Nabors, L. A., & Kichler, J. C. (2015). An Evaluation of a Juvenile Idiopathic Arthritis Retreat for Families. *Pediatric Rheumatology*, 13(1), 12 (5 pages). DOI 10.1186/s12969-015-0010-3.

Merianos, A. L., Vidourek, R. A., King, K. A., & Nabors, L. A. (2015). Hospital, school, and community-based strategies to enhance the quality of life of youth with chronic illnesses. *Applied Research in Quality of Life,* 10, 329–342. DOI 10.1007/s11482-014-9311-9.

Merianos, A. L., King, K. A., Vidourek, R. A., & Nabors, L. A. (2015 epub ahead of print). Mentoring and Peer-led Interventions to Improve Quality of Life Outcomes among Adolescents with Chronic Illnesses. *Applied Research in Quality of Life*, 1-15.

Nabors, L., Ige. J. T., Fevrier, B., (2015). Peer Support and Psychosocial Pain Management Strategies for Children with Systemic Lupus Erythematosus. *Journal of Immunology Research*, epub no. 238263, pp. 1-5.

Nabors, L. A., Merianos, A. L., & Olsen, B. (in press). Perceptions of a child who was overweight or average weight by African American children. *Child and Adolescent Social Work Journal.*

Merianos, A. L., King, K. A., Vidourek, R. A., & Nabors, L. A. (in press). School experiences associated with alcohol use among Hispanic youth. *Journal of School Health.*

Nabors, L. & Dai, C-L. (in press). Forward: Linkages among Traumatic Experiences and Psychosocial Factors and Ecological Outcomes for Children and Adolescents. *Journal of Prevention and Intervention in the Community.*

Nabors, L., Baker-Phibbs, C., & Burbage, M. (in press). Predictors of Child Functioning and Problem Behaviors for Children Diagnosed with Post-Traumatic Stress Disorder and Externalizing Problems. *Journal of Prevention and Intervention in the Community.*

Nabors, L., Baker-Phibbs, C., & Woodson, K. (in press). Community-based Counselors' Interventions for Elementary School-Age Children Coping with Trauma. *Journal of Prevention and Intervention in the Community.*

Nabors, L. A., Merianos, A. L., Vidourek, R. A., King, K. A., Rosen, B. L., Zhang, J., & Swoboda, C. (in press). Predictors of Flourishing for Adolescents with Asthma. *Journal of Asthma.*

In: Marijuana
Editor: Margie Vasquez

ISBN: 978-1-63484-409-3

Chapter 4

LEGALIZATION AND THE EFFECT ON YOUTH: ARTICULATING A CLEAR AND EFFECTIVE MARIJUANA POLICY

Stephen M. Miller*
Claremont Graduate University,
Claremont Graduate University, Claremont, CA, US

ABSTRACT

In the past decade, Americans have seen public opinion towards marijuana shift from a majority opposed to a majority in favor of making the substance legal for recreational use. Despite federal laws maintaining a strict prohibition of marijuana as a schedule 1 drug, nearly half of all states have legalized marijuana for medical use, while others have taken the unprecedented step of legalizing marijuana for recreational use as well. However, due to the federal restriction on funds for marijuana research, evidence for the long term effects of marijuana use is lacking. The limited research that does exist concerning the effects of marijuana on children is as diverse and conflicted as drug policy itself, with some studies suggesting a risk of permanent cognitive impairment (Meier et al., 2012), while others find no linkage between adolescent marijuana use and physical or mental health problems in adulthood (Bechtold et al., 2015). Issues of commercialization juxtaposed against similarities and

* Corresponding Author: Stephen Miller, Email: Stephen.miller@cgu.edu. Tel: 323-404-3294. Fax: 909-621-5221.

differences to tobacco and alcohol are at the forefront of concerns surrounding the impact on adolescent use. Policy makers must consider how evolving laws and social norms may affect adolescent experimentation and uptake. This commentary will examine the issues surrounding legalization and teen use and the policy steps that might be taken to effectively communicate the risks to adolescents amidst an ever more socially acceptable climate.

INTRODUCTION

At the time of this writing 23 states (and Washington D.C.) had legalized medical marijuana and 4 states had approved the sale of marijuana for recreational use. This is astonishing as less than 20 years ago the drug was not available (legally) in any state, for any purpose. It seems American society, and with it public opinion, is significantly less opposed to legalization since the days of "Reefer Madness." The most recent polling data shows that 84% of Americans think marijuana should be legal for medical uses and 53% approve of its use recreationally (CBS News Poll, 2015). Proponents of legalization argue it is only a matter of time before marijuana is legally available nationwide, while the opposition still warns against the negative ramifications a lifting of the national prohibition would bring. Chief among them is the effect legalization will have on youth experimentation and uptake. Much like alcohol, states that have legalized marijuana have restricted its sale to persons 21 years old or older. However, the concern is that as marijuana becomes more widely available, youth usage rates will rise. Over the past 40 years adolescent marijuana use remained largely stagnant; however, the most recent evidence suggests experimentation and use are on the rise (Lanza, Vasilenko, Dziak, & Butera, 2015). This brief commentary is meant to bring attention to the relevant issues surrounding the relationship between marijuana legalization and its effect on youth. Whether one is for or against the legalization of marijuana (medically and/or recreationally) it is worth considering the effect on youth, especially the unintended consequences that may be mitigated by effective control policy.

On first blush, the potential legalization of marijuana may seem to solve more problems than it causes. After all, to remove prohibition means less activities constitute crimes while the government has more authority to regulate commerce as a licit controlled substance. With respect to minors, one could even argue that nothing really changes at all, because marijuana would still be illegal for children to purchase and consume. However, such a simplistic perspective on legalization fails to realize the "unintended consequences" that legalization may portend. From a psychological standpoint, legalization reflects a societal norm that marijuana use is both acceptable and safe (Friese, & Grube, 2013). Minors may view such a policy shift as a "green light" to experiment with marijuana, as many currently do with alcohol and tobacco (Hawkins, Catalano, & Miller, 1992). In support of this proposition, a recent study found that adolescents who were non-users expressed greater intentions to experiment with marijuana in the future while users were more likely to increase their use if it were to become legal (Palamar, Ompad, & Petkova, 2014). These are just some of the issues that suggest it is naïve to presuppose the legalization of marijuana will not have an effect on youth.

A critic of the above arguments might respond with an emphatic, "So what!?" Pro arguments consistently claim that, as a drug, marijuana is far safer than alcohol or tobacco (e.g., Lachenmeier, & Rehm, 2015). To this point, the term "safer" must be taken with a grain of salt. Because one drug is "safer" than another drug does not mean that the drug is "safe." This is especially true in the case of adolescent substance use, which in turn speaks to the broader case for prohibition of use by minors. While the reasons for prohibition of substance use by minors are numerous, they can be summarized by two main arguments, 1.) Minors lack the maturity and self-control (executive functioning development) to use controlled substances responsibly, and 2.) Young adults' brains are still developing and the introduction of psychoactive chemicals could permanently delay brain development. The second point is particularly germane to the "safe" argument. Currently, the research on the longitudinal effects of adolescent marijuana use is both sparse and conflicting. Meier and colleagues (2012) found that early, persistent marijuana use by teenagers was linked to an increased risk of permanent cognitive impairment. Yet another study found no relation between marijuana use in adolescence and physical or mental health problems later in life (Bechtold et al., 2015). Of particular concern is the potency of the marijuana available today. In 1975 the average THC content of cannabis based products available in the United States was 0.74%, but by 2008 that number had risen to 8.8%, with some products rating as highly as 29.3% (ElSohly, Holley, & Turner, 1985; Mehmedic et al., 2010). Increased potency combined with use by adolescents while their brains are still developing has the potential to foster addictive tendencies (Volkow, Baler, Compton, & Weiss, 2014), a consequence once thought impossible from regular marijuana use. For these reasons and more a clearly articulated marijuana control policy should be in place to protect children from the harms of drug use.

But what can be done? There are at least four steps that local and state (and perhaps federal) governments can take to protect adolescents from the dangers of marijuana use even as the drug is legalized for adult recreational use. The first step is to effectively communicate what legalization of a controlled substance means on a societal level. It took a long, LONG time before the public was able to distinguish between tobacco being legal and tobacco not being "safe." Eventually though, effective and persistent public health campaigns have clearly articulated the dangers of smoking and as a result smoking rates have steadily declined over the past 50 years for adults and 15 years for youth (CDC, 2011). From a public health communication standpoint, we should be cautious to avoid the mistakes of the past, exaggerating the negative effects of marijuana use (e.g., "Reefer Madness) or relying on non-evidence based anti-drug campaigns (e.g., DARE). Instead, public health officials should partner with psychologists and communication experts to clearly present the case against marijuana use by adolescents.

The second step relates to the potential commercialization of marijuana. Countless studies show that exposure to marketing (e.g., tobacco marketing) has a pernicious effect on youth (Agaku, & Ayo-Yusuf, 2014; Fulmer et al., 2015; Sargent, Gibson, & Heatherton, 2009) and that they are exposed to such marketing practices constantly (Henriksen, Feighery, Schleicher, Haladjian, & Fortmann, 2004). Putting restrictions on the degree to which marijuana is commercialized should limit how youth are exposed to the substance and subsequent desires to experiment with the drug. This means a complete moratorium on radio and television ads, no billboards, and limiting print advertising to publications that cannot be sold to anyone under the age of 21. Further, marijuana dispensaries should not be located anywhere near K-12 schools as these areas are naturally frequented more often by youth. It is one thing to legalize a substance and quite another to normalize its use via a constant barrage of commercial advertising.

The third step concerns law enforcement policies, specifically as they pertain to youth. Currently, marijuana is legal for recreational and/or medical use in only some of the states, while still illegal for sale or purchase federally. In the states where marijuana has been legalized, law enforcement officials should make it a priority to rigorously enforce the prohibition on stores selling to minors. In addition, they can focus efforts on preventing "straw purchases" to reduce the ways in which minors can gain access to marijuana. And finally, when confronted with adolescents who are caught in possession of marijuana, law enforcement personnel should focus on working with the children to identify the source of the drug rather than on merely punishing the offenders. In sum, the focus of law enforcement should switch from punishment to prevention in the interest of the greater goal of harm reduction.

The fourth and perhaps most crucial step that can be taken is to engage parents in the larger debate of how legalization might have an impact on their own children. This should be done primarily to inform parents of their role in preventing illegal adolescent marijuana use. Studies have shown consistently that parental monitoring is an effective deterrent of adolescent marijuana use (Lac & Crano, 2009). Further, parents should be given the necessary information and strategies to talk to children about the difference between legalization and "safe" or acceptable uses. As with alcohol, parents should take on the responsibility of discussing why a substance is legal for adults but illegal for children, while at the same time communicating the expectations they have for their children.

CONCLUSION

A reader of this commentary might conclude that the author is opposed to legalization, which is both untrue and beside the point. Indeed, there are positive aspects to legalization that should be conceded. To start, laws should reflect the society over which they govern and as public sentiment shifts laws may be adjusted accordingly. The lesson of prohibition taught us that unenforceable laws that do not have popular support serve only to breed contempt for the law which undermines a country's ability to police itself. On a related point, the criminal justice system would no longer be burdened by the countless individuals imprisoned for what most Americans consider a harmless vice. Legalization of marijuana provides an opportunity for governments and families to have an open conversation with youth about a widely available drug that may pose real risks to adolescent health. If one believes, as I do, that it is the responsibility of society to protect children from harm, then we should take this opportunity to talk to children about what legalization means and how substance use relates to their own health and well-being. Too often momentum builds for a movement that, when advanced, fails to address the potential unintended consequences following the aftermath of change. I believe it is the responsibility of both advocates and opponents of legalization to consider the impact on children and the ways in which negative consequences can be prevented or at the very least mitigated. The recommendations presented here are an entreaty to engage in a larger discussion of the impact of the legalization of marijuana on adolescent use. Ultimately, the goal should be to establish a well-articulated marijuana control policy that reflects a growing shift in public opinion while simultaneously protects our children from harm.

ACKNOWLEDGMENTS

I would like to thank Dr. William Crano for his comments on this chapter.

REFERENCES

Agaku, I. T., & Ayo-Yusuf, O. A. (2014). The effect of exposure to pro-tobacco advertising on experimentation with emerging tobacco products among U.S. Adolescents. *Health Education & Behavior*, *41*(3), 275-280. doi:10.1177/1090198113511817.

Bechtold, J., Simpson, T., White, H. R., & Pardini, D. (2015). Chronic Adolescent Marijuana Use as a Risk Factor for Physical and Mental Health Problems in Young Adult Men. *Psychology of Addictive Behaviors*, doi:10.1037/adb0000103.

CBS News Poll. April 8-12, 2015. N = 1,012 adults nationwide. Margin of error +- 3. Retrieved from: http://www.pollingreport.com/drugs.htm.

CDC. (2011). Trends in Current Cigarette Smoking Among High School Students and Adults, United States, 1965-2011. Retrieved from: http://www.cdc.gov/tobacco/data_statistics/tables/trends/cig_smoking/.

ElSohly MA, Holley JH, Turner CE. Constituents of Cannabis sativa L. XXVI. The D9 -tetrahydrocannabinol content of confiscated marijuana, 1974–1983. In: Harvey DJ, Paton W, Nahas GG, editors. Marijuana '84: proceedings of the Oxford symposium on cannabis. England: IRL Press, 1985;37–42.

Friese, B., & Grube, J. W. (2013). Legalization of medical marijuana and marijuana use among youths. *Drugs: Education, Prevention & Policy*, *20*(1), 33-39. doi:10.3109/09687637.2012.713408.

Fulmer, E. B., Neilands, T. B., Dube, S. R., Kuiper, N. M., Arrazola, R. A., & Glantz, S. A. (2015). Protobacco media exposure and youth susceptibility to smoking cigarettes, cigarette experimentation, and current tobacco use among US youth. *Plos ONE, 10*(8).

Hawkins, J. D., Catalano, R. F., & Miller, J. Y. (1992). Risk and protective factors for alcohol and other drug problems in adolescence and early adulthood: Implications for substance abuse prevention. *Psychological Bulletin, 112*(1), 64-105. doi:10.1037/0033-2909.112.1.64.

Henriksen, L., Feighery, E. C., Schleicher, N. C., Haladjian, H. H., & Fortmann, S. P. (2004). Reaching youth at the point of sale: cigarette marketing is more prevalent in stores where adolescents shop frequently. *Tobacco Control, 13*, 315-318. DOI: 10.1136/tc.2003.006577.

Lac, A. & Crano, W. D. (2009). Monitoring matters: Meta-analytic review reveals the reliable linkage of parental monitoring with adolescent marijuana use. Perspectives on Psychological Science, 4, 578-86.

Lachenmeier, D. W., & Rehm, J. (2015). Comparative risk assessment of alcohol, tobacco, cannabis and other illicit drugs using the margin of exposure approach. *Scientific Reports, 5* doi: 10.1038/srep08126.

Lanza, S. T., Vasilenko, S. A., Dziak, J. J., & Butera, N. M. (2015). Trends among US high school seniors in recent marijuana use and associations with other substances: 1976 to 2013. *Journal of Adolescent Health, 57, 198-204*.

Mehmedic, Z., Chandra, S., Slade, D., Denham, H., Foster, S., Patel, A. S., & ElSohly, M. A. (2010). Potency trends of Δ^9-THC and other cannabinoids in confiscated cannabis preparations from 1993 to 2008. *Journal of Forensic Sciences, 55*(5), 1209-1217. doi:10.1111/j.1556-4029.2010.01441.x.

Meier, M. H., Caspi, A., Ambler, A., Harrington, H., Houts, R., Keefe, R. E., & Moffitt, T. E. (2012). Persistent cannabis users show neuropsychological decline from childhood to midlife. PNAS Proceedings of the National Academy of Sciences of the United States of America, *109*(40), E2657-E2664. doi:10.1073/pnas.1206820109.

Palamar, J. J., Ompad, D. C., & Petkova, E. (2014). Correlates of intentions to use cannabis among US high school seniors in the case of cannabis legalization. *International Journal of Drug Policy, 25*(3), 424-435. doi:10.1016/j.drugpo.2014.01.017.

Sargent, J. D., Gibson, J., & Heatherton, T. F. (2009). Comparing the effects of entertainment media and tobacco marketing on youth smoking. *Tobacco Control: An International Journal, 18*(1), 47-53. doi:10.1136/tc.2008.026153.

Volkow, N. D., Baler, R. D., Compton, W. M., & Weiss, S. R. (2014). Adverse Health Effects of Marijuana Use. *The New England Journal of Medicine*, 370, 2219-2227. doi: 10.1056/NEJMra1402309.

BIOGRAPHICAL SKETCH

Name: Stephen M. Miller
Affiliation: Claremont Graduate University
Date of Birth: 11/08/1980
Education:

Claremont Graduate University	Claremont, CA
Ph.D. Candidate, Social Psychology	expected 5-16
Claremont Graduate University	Claremont, CA
M.A., Social Psychology	5-11

Emphasis: Health Behavior, Evaluation

Claremont McKenna College	Claremont, CA
B.A., Psychology & History	5-03

Address:

123 E. 8th St.
Claremont, CA 91711

Research and Professional Experience:

Over the past several years I have conducted a series of research projects as a member of the Health Psychology and Prevention Science Institute at Claremont Graduate University. My work is generally focused on how prior social experiences motivate health behaviors in individuals. Previous work includes authoring a grant funded publication using data from the National Survey of Parents and Youth on the relationship between parent and child marijuana use. A recent book chapter focuses on how parental behavior influences child marijuana initiation. I am currently engaged in research on the psychological constructs linking previous participation in organized youth sports with adult levels of physical activity.

Professionally, I have worked in the American Psychological Association's Public Interest Government Relations Office on issues related to: health disparities in mental health access, juvenile justice, and the effect of sequestration on vulnerable populations. Prior to that, I worked on an NIH funded research project on childhood obesity. For this project I coordinated an fMRI sub study on the neurocognitive correlates of dietary inhibition in adolescents. Currently, I am employed as a research assistant working on an R01 funded project related to nicotine and tobacco uptake in a population of at-risk youth.

Professional Appointments: None

Honors:

Dean's Competitive Travel Award (3x) (Claremont Graduate University)

Recipient: Merit-Based Fellowship (Claremont Graduate University)

Recipient: Dean's Merit Award (Claremont Graduate University)

John Stauffer Fellow (Claremont Graduate University)

Publications Last 3 Years:

Miller, S. M., Siegel, J. T., & Crano, W. D. (in press). Parent's Influence on Their Children's Cannabis Use. In: *The Handbook of Cannabis and Related Pathologies: Biology, Diagnosis, Treatment and Pharmacology*. Preedy, Victor R. (Ed); London: Elsevier.

Miller, S. M., Siegel, J. T., Hohman, Z., & Crano, W. D. (2013). Factors mediating the association of the recency of parent's marijuana use and their adolescent children's subsequent initiation. *Psychology Of Addictive Behaviors*, *27*(3), 848-853. doi:10.1037/a0032201.

In: Marijuana
Editor: Margie Vasquez

ISBN: 978-1-63484-409-3

Chapter 5

HEALTH AND SAFETY WARNINGS FOR LEGALLY SOLD MARIJUANA

John M. Malouff
University of New England, Australia

INTRODUCTION

This chapter covers the recent rise of legally sold marijuana, the risks of marijuana use, arguments in support of mandating warnings on packages of legally sold marijuana, the likely benefits and costs of mandating warnings, ways of evaluating proposed and actual warnings, and specific recommended warnings. The chapter also describes a court-imposed duty to warn as a possible alternative to legislatively or administratively-mandated warnings.

Legalizing the Sale of Marijuana

In recent decades some governments have legalized the use of marijuana for medical purposes. At present, 20 states and the District of Columbia allow the growing and sale of medical marijuana: Alaska, Arizona, California, Colorado, Connecticut, Delaware, Hawaii, Illinois, Maine, Massachusetts, Michigan, Montana, Nevada, New Hampshire, New Jersey, New Mexico, Oregon, Rhode Island, Vermont, and Washington (New Health Guide, 2015). Countries that allow the sale of medical marijuana include Canada, the Czech

Republic, and France (New Health Guide, 2015). Other states and nations are considering legalizing medical marijuana (Cheat Sheet, 2015; Medical Marijuana, 2015).

Recently, four U.S. states (Alaska, Colorado, Oregon, and Washington) and the District of Columbia, legalized leisure marijuana growing and sale (Governing the States and Localities, 2015). There are movements in several other states also to legalize leisure marijuana (Becker, 2015). The federal government still bans marijuana, but it has decided, at least for the time being, not to prosecute individuals who follow the law in those states that legalize it for medical or leisure use (Reilly & Grim, 2013; Stout & Moore, 2009). Uruguay has also recently legalized leisure marijuana (McKay, 2014).

Risks of Marijuana Use

Using marijuana creates many health and safety risks. The Surgeon General of the United States (U.S. Department of Health and Human Services, 1982) issued the following statement in 1982:

Among the known or suspected chronic effects of marijuana are:

1. short-term memory impairment and slowness of learning.
2. impaired lung function similar to that found in cigarette smokers. Indications are that more serious effects, such as cancer and other lung disease, follow extended use.
3. decreased sperm count and sperm motility.
4. interference with ovulation and pre-natal development.
5. impaired immune response.
6. possible adverse effects on heart function.
7. by-products of marijuana remaining in body fat for several weeks, with unknown consequences. The storage of these by-products increases the possiblilties [sic] for chronic, as well as residual, effects on performance, even after the acute reaction to the drug has worn off. Of special concern are the long-term developmental effects in children and adolescents, who are particularly vulnerable to the drug's behavioral and psychological effects. The “amotivational syndrome,” characterized by a pattern of energy loss, diminished school performance, harmed parental relationships, and other behavioral disruptions, has been associated with prolonged marijuana use by young persons.

Studies have produced evidence of many risks of marijuana use. The most recent reviews of this evidence (Danovitch, 2012; Hill, 2015; Volkow, Baler, Compton, & Weiss, 2014), indicate that marijuana is associated with *acute effects* such as (1) impaired memory, motor coordination, and judgment; (2) impaired driving; and (3) paranoia and psychosis; along with *long-term-use effects* of (4) structural changes in brain structures, (5) addiction, (6) withdrawal, including dysphoria, craving, and insomnia, upon ceasing use, (7) problems in work, school, and relationships, (8) mental health problems including anxiety, depression, and psychosis, (9) unemployment, decreased income, and criminal behavior, (10) lung disease, (11) heart disease, (12) stroke, and (13) fetal harm. Special risks may arise with use of high-potency (high THC) types of marijuana (Volkow et al., 2014) and use of edible marijuana (Centers for Disease Control and Prevention, 2015).

Causation is not completely clear for all these risks, as third variables, including genetic factors and the use of other drugs, such as tobacco, might contribute to both marijuana use and some health problems (Volkow et al., 2014). Further, it is possible that risks vary to some extent from person to person, depending on genetic and other individual risk factors. These individual differences could explain sudden deaths that seem due to marijuana use (Stuart & Wing, 2014).

Many of the health and safety risks of marijuana are similar to those of alcohol or tobacco, for instance dangers associated with operating a motor vehicle while under the influence, fetal harm, and the risk of heart disease (Malouff & Rooke, 2013). Little research has been done on adverse interactions of marijuana and other drugs, but the potent effects of marijuana suggest that drug interactions could occur. Although marijuana use, unlike cocaine and heroin use, does not seem to create a significant risk of sudden death, overdosing, e.g., through eating too much (Pandey, 2015) or using high THC brands, can lead to a greater risk of short-term side-effects than one might expect.

Arguments for Government-Mandated Marijuana Warnings

Legal marijuana occupies a unique domain of no mandated warnings for users of a dangerous product. That situation cannot last long.

Arguments for government-mandated warnings on legally sold packages of marijuana include that the government has a duty to take actions to protect the health of its citizens; equity requires that parallels to other dangerous drugs, including leisure drugs such as alcohol and tobacco, and medical drugs, such as psychiatric drugs, lead to government-mandated marijuana warnings; warnings on product packages have positive effects; and mandating warnings on marijuana packages would involve little cost for government, sellers, or consumers. Virtually no one would argue about the duty of government to protect the health of its citizens. The following sections focus on precedents for marijuana warnings, likely effects of the warnings, and the cost of mandating warnings.

Precedents for Marijuana Warnings

Tobacco Warnings

Many countries have mandated specific warnings on tobacco packages (Tobacco Labeling Resource Centre, 2013). The warnings vary between smoked and smokeless tobacco due to different risks. The warnings also vary from country to country, with some countries mandating graphic (gruesome) images of harm that can be caused by tobacco use, e.g., gangrenous toes, oral cancer, and being unable to breath (Australian Government Department of Health, 2014).

Alcohol Warnings

Several nations mandate warnings on alcohol containers (World Health Organization, 2015). The sole mandated warning in the U.S. is: "GOVERNMENT WARNING: (1) According to the Surgeon General, women should not drink alcoholic beverages during pregnancy because of the risk of birth defects. (2) Consumption of alcoholic beverages impairs your ability to drive a car or operate machinery, and may cause health problems." (U. S. Code of Federal Regulations, 2015).

Prescription and Over-the-Counter Drugs

In the U.S., the Food and Drug Administration (FDA) mandates warnings where there are significant risks associated with use. For instance, the FDA required acetaminophen manufacturers to warn users of various health risks, including rare but possibly deadly skin reactions (Cleveland Clinic, 2014). In some cases, the drug manufacturer provides warnings to reduce its risk of liability for failure to warn of known dangers. Many drugs, including psychiatric medications and certain anti-inflammatory drugs, have these warnings. For instance, one small part of the physician warning regarding Xanax (Pfizer, 2013) states:

> Certain adverse clinical events, some life-threatening, are a direct consequence of physical dependence to XANAX. These include a spectrum of withdrawal symptoms; the most important is seizure. Even after relatively shortterm [sic] use at the doses recommended for the treatment of transient anxiety and anxiety disorder (i.e., 0.75 to 4.0 mg per day), there is some risk of dependence.

The warning goes on to mentions risks of fetal harm, unsafe driving, and dangerous interactions with specific other drugs

Effects of Health Warnings on Products

Studies have shown that smokers consider tobacco warnings effective, that the warnings increase awareness of risks, and that smoking decreases when prominent warnings are introduced (Hammond, 2011), as shown most recently by the major drop in tobacco consumption and interest in smoking initiation in Australia after the introduction of plain brown packages, each with a gruesome image of harm that tobacco can cause (Tanquintic-Misa, 2015).

Not many studies have examined the impact of alcohol warnings. At present, there is no solid evidence that warnings on alcohol containers reduce alcohol abuse; however, there is evidence that they lead to an increase in awareness of drinking-related risks (Wilkinson & Room, 2009). Wilkinson and Room (2009) speculated that the single U.S. alcohol warning may have limited effects on behavior because the warning is not rotated, is vague, and is not vividly presented. Research evidence indicates that the warning is inconspicuous (Malouff, Gabrilowitz, & Schutte, 1992).

The effects of mandated warnings on prescription and over-the-counter drugs are not known. It is likely that they raise awareness, to the extent that they are read and understood. Ensuring awareness of risks is the primary intent of those warnings.

Costs of Mandated Warnings

Deciding what warnings to mandate could be costly for a state. Hence, it might make sense for a group of states to combine in creating a list of warnings from which each state could choose. The actual placing of warnings on marijuana packages would cost little. The packages typically have printed brand information on them anyway. If tobacco warnings are any model (see Armitage, 2014), one might wonder whether the most significant cost for governments might be defending lawsuits filed by marijuana companies. However, legal marijuana producers do not at present have the huge amounts of money of tobacco companies to prosecute lawsuits. Further, in some cases, marijuana producers could be court-ordered to pay the expenses of the government when the government prevails in a lawsuit. Finally, marijuana producers would not want to bite the hand that feeds them. Governments that legalized marijuana could make it illegal again or raise related fees or taxes.

Warnings on marijuana packages would likely increase awareness of risks. Effects on behavior might depend on how prominent and emotion-arousing the warnings are.

WHAT MARIJUANA WARNINGS TO MANDATE

Previously Recommended Marijuana Warnings

Malouff and Rooke (2013) asked world-leading marijuana researchers what they would suggest as government-mandated warnings on legally sold marijuana packages. The experts suggested (p. 93):

> *Safety*. Using marijuana can increase your risk of driving accidents and accidents in any other activity that requires your full attention and motor skills.
>
> *Physical health*. Using marijuana can cause lung and heart problems.
>
> *Fetal harm*. Avoid using cannabis if you may become pregnant, and avoid cannabis use while pregnant, as use may harm the fetus physically and lead to psychopathology later in life.
>
> *Mental health*. Using marijuana can cause serious harm to your mental health.
>
> *Drug dependence*. Using marijuana can lead to dependence and withdrawal.

> *Negative effects on development.* Adolescents using marijuana may experience deficiencies in brain development and more difficulties in succeeding in life.

Malouff, Johnson, and Rooke (2015) then asked marijuana users to provide warnings they would suggest if the government mandated warnings on marijuana packages. The suggestions, based mostly on the personal experiences and observations of the users, overlapped to a large extent with those of the experts, but also included two warnings that might be particularly within the knowledge of users:

> *Marijuana use can cause short-term physical side-effects.* "May induce drowsiness." "May cause dizziness and disorientation." "This drug may cause feelings of nausea."
>
> *Use responsibly.* "Follow dosing instructions on package." "Use responsibly." "To be used in moderation."

Choosing Marijuana Warnings to Mandate

If governments mandate warnings through legislation or administrative rule making, the question becomes what warnings to mandate. This question could become highly political as legal marijuana producers become big enough to hire lobbyists and make campaign donations to elected officials. Their interests might suggest minimal warnings. Health professionals, many of whom oppose legalization, might lobby for maximum warnings, including gruesome images on otherwise plain packages, as Australia now mandates for tobacco packages (Australian Government Department of Health, 2014). Because marijuana is used as a medicine by some individuals, it would seem inappropriate to mandate gruesome images. However, some experts might disagree with this point of view. A plain packaging rule would be appropriate to help limit promotion of a dangerous product. Mandating several warnings that are rotated for equal distribution, as is done with tobacco products in the United States (Centers for Disease Control and Prevention, 2000), would seem appropriate because there are many potential warnings and packages of marijuana are often small. It is important to mandate also the size of the warning words (see e.g., Cornel University Law School Legal Information Institute, n.d.). Malouff, Schutte, Wiener, Brancazio, and Fish (1993) evaluated the U.S.-mandated alcohol warnings on actual containers and concluded that they did not meet the statutory requirement of being "conspicuous."

The content of the warnings could include some form of the eight warnings suggested in total by experts and users (Malouff & Rooke, 2013; Malouff et al., 2015). These are:

1. Using marijuana can increase your risk of driving accidents and accidents in any other activity that requires your full attention and motor skills.
2. Using marijuana can cause lung and heart problems.
3. Avoid using cannabis if you may become pregnant, and avoid cannabis use while pregnant, as use may harm the fetus physically and lead to psychopathology later in life.
4. Using marijuana can cause serious harm to your mental health.
5. Using marijuana can lead to dependence and withdrawal.
6. Marijuana use can cause short-term physical side-effects, including drowsiness, dizziness, disorientation, and nausea.
7. Adolescents using marijuana may experience deficiencies in brain development and more difficulties in succeeding in life.
8. Follow dosing instructions on package and use responsibly.

New risk-relevant information might come to light as time passes, through either research findings or incident reports. For instance, studies of marijuana vaporizers suggest that they are safer than smoked marijuana, due to the absence of combustion products (Earleywine & Van Dam, 2010; Malouff, Rooke, & Copeland, 2014; Van Dam & Earleywine, 2010). A surprising incident of sudden death after use of eaten marijuana (Centers for Disease Control and Prevention, 2015) indicated a new sort of risk. The warning process needs to be flexible enough to include risk-related information supported convincingly by evidence in the future.

Evaluating Proposed and Actual Marijuana Warnings

It would be sensible to empirically evaluate various aspects of potential warnings. There are methods of assessing the reading level needed to understand a sentence. Malouff, Gabrilowitz et al., (1992) did that with U.S.

tobacco and alcohol warnings. Lower demands for reading ability would be best, all else being equal. There are ways to evaluate important characteristics of proposed warnings, e.g., with focus groups or in survey research targeting users, potential users, marijuana experts, and marijuana industry representatives. Important characteristics for warnings, in addition to readability, include that the targeted individuals tend to notice, read, believe, remember, and consider personally relevant the warnings. Malouff, Schutte, Frohardt, Deming, and Mantelli (1992) evaluated these sorts of characteristics regarding American tobacco warnings. Habituation to warnings could lower the impact of the effects (regarding habituation to tobacco warnings, see Rooke, Malouff, & Copeland, 2012).

Duty to Warn as an Alternative to Specific Government-Mandated Warnings

In addition to legislation or administrative rule making, governments might in essence mandate warnings through court decisions in product liability cases involving failure to warn of risks of marijuana use. "A manufacturer has a duty to provide an adequate warning to the user on how to use the product if a reasonably foreseeable use of the product involves a substantial danger of which the manufacturer either is aware or should be aware, and that would not be readily recognized by the ordinary user." *Greenman v. Yuba Power Products, Inc.* (1963). The risk of harm must be non-obvious, so knife makers need not warn that a knife can cut a person if not used carefully. In the case of prescription drugs, U.S. courts follow the "learned intermediary rule" which states that it is the duty of pharmaceutical companies to warn doctors and pharmacists rather than users (Johnson, Donahue, & Sarti, 2013). The purpose of this rule is that a learned professional is needed to explain risks to specific users. Courts could apply the rule to medical marijuana. That would be an extension of the rule because the physicians who approve individuals to use medical marijuana typically do not actually prescribe it. If the rule were applied, however, the physicians could be liable in damages for failure to warn of non-obvious risks about which they reasonably should have warned an individual. The approving physicians might be better off with government-mandated warnings on packages.

In the case of legal leisure marijuana, there typically is no physician prescribing or approving use. Hence, there could be no application of the learned intermediary rule. Marijuana producers have a duty to warn users about non-obvious risks of which they know or should reasonably know. The recommended warnings listed above would seem to fit in this category, although a producer-defendant could try to prove that the person actually knew of the risk. Pharmaceutical companies are presumed by courts to be experts on their drugs and to keep up with research findings showing risks. Courts might expect less expertise from marijuana producers, but if the producers have sales revenues in the millions of dollars, courts might also expect them to keep up to date on research findings relating to health and safety risks created by use of their product.

If a court found failure to warn in a case, it would then award money damages caused by the failure. These damages might cover costs relating to medical treatment, loss of wages while unable to work, permanent disability or death, and so on. The plaintiff would have to prove by preponderance of the evidence that a warning would have prevented the harm. That could be difficult if the injured individual had used marijuana extensively before buying the defendant's marijuana. Also, use of marijuana from multiple producers might make it difficult to prove which marijuana caused the harm. The best case for a plaintiff would be a naïve, first-time purchaser who has a bad trip and suffers a grievous injury as a result, say, of paranoid behavior.

A judgment in favor of a plaintiff in a case based on failure to warn would not impose a mandate on legal marijuana producers, but it would create widespread concern among them about being the subject of future damage awards. As a practical matter, most or all marijuana producers in the state or nation would then start providing written warnings just as pharmaceutical companies do for over-the-counter drugs that carry a significant risk of harm.

Conclusion

Legislative or administrative mandating of warnings on marijuana products requires a certain level of political will. That political will might develop as a result of deadly incidents involving marijuana use, continuing increases in marijuana-related tax revenues, or political pressure from public health professionals or anti-drug groups. Dissemination of information such as in this chapter might also contribute.

Judicial pressures on marijuana producers to warn must await lawsuits based on failure to warn, possibly about the risks mentioned above. Research showing that marijuana users are not aware of certain risks could help provide an empirical basis for such lawsuits, as well as for legislatively or administratively-mandated warnings.

REFERENCES

Armitage, J. (2014). Big tobacco puts countries on trial as concerns over TTIP deals mount. *The Independent.* Retrieved from http://www.independent.co.uk/news/business/analysis-and-features/big-tobacco-puts-countries-on-trial-as-concerns-over-ttip-deals-mount-9807478.html.

Australian Government Department of Health. (2014). *Introduction of tobacco plain packaging in Australia.* Retrieved from http://www.health.gov.au/internet/main/publishing.nsf/content/tobacco-plain.

Becker, S. (2015, June 19). 7 states on the verge of marijuana legalization. *The Cheat Sheet.* Retrieved July 22, 2015, from http://www.cheatsheet.com/business/5-states-and-one-city-ready-to-legalize-arijuana.html/?a=viewall.

Centers for Disease Control and Prevention. (2000). *Smoking & tobacco use.* Retrieved from http://www.cdc.gov/tobacco/data_statistics/sgr/2000/highlights/labels/.

Centers for Disease Control and Prevention. (2015). *Notes from the field: Death following ingestion of an edible marijuana product – Colorado, March 2014.* Retrieved from http://www.cdc.gov/mmwr/preview/mmwrhtml/mm6428a6.htm.

Cheat Sheet. (2015, May 22). *Legalization.* Retrieved September 4, 2015, from http://www.cheatsheet.com/politics/10-countries-that-have-or-will-see-marijuana-legalization.html/?a=viewall.

Cleveland Clinic. (2014, January 27). *FDA mandates new acetaminophen warning.* Retrieved from http://health.clevelandclinic.org/2014/01/fda-mandates-new-acetaminophen-warning/.

Cornel University Law School Legal Information Institute. (n.d.). *15 U.S. Code Chapter 70 – Comprehensive Smokeless Tobacco Health Education.* Retrieved from https://www.law.cornell.edu/uscode/text/15/chapter-70.

Danovitch, I. (2012). Sorting through the science on marijuana: Facts, fallacies, and implications for legalization. *McGeorge Law Review, 43,* 91-108.

Earleywine, M. & Van Dam, N. T. (2010). Case studies in cannabis vaporization. *Addiction Research & Theory, 18,* 243-249.

Governing the States and Localities. (2015). *State marijuana laws map*. Retrieved from http://www.governing.com/gov-data/state-marijuana-laws-map-medical-recreational.html.

Greenman v. Yuba Power Products, Inc. (1963). 59 Cal.2d 57, 13 A.L.R.3d 1049.

Hammond, D. (2011). Health warning messages on tobacco products: A review. *Tobacco Control*, *20*, 327-337.

Hill, K. P. (2015). Medical marijuana for treatment of chronic pain and other medical and psychiatric problems: A clinical review. *JAMA*, *313*, 2474-2483.

Johnson, C. A., Donahue, A. J. & Sarti, P. (2013). Inside the learned intermediary doctrine. *American Bar Association*. Retrieved from http://apps.americanbar.org/litigation/committees/products/articles/summer2013-0713-inside-learned-intermediary-doctrine.html.

Malouff, J., Gabrilowitz, D. & Schutte, N. (1992). Readability of health warnings on alcohol and tobacco products. *American Journal of Public Health*, *82*, 464.

Malouff, J. M., Johnson, C. E. & Rooke, S. E. (2015). Marijuana users' recommended warnings for packages of legally sold marijuana. Manuscript submitted for publication.

Malouff, J. M. & Rooke, S. E. (2013). Expert-recommended warnings for medical marijuana. *Substance Abuse*, *34*, 92-93.

Malouff, J. M., Rooke, S. E. & Copeland, J. (2014). Experiences of marijuana-vaporizer users. *Substance Abuse*, *35*, 127-128.

Malouff, J., Schutte, N., Frohardt, M., Deming, W. & Mantelli, D. (1992). Preventing smoking: Evaluating the potential effectiveness of cigarette warnings. *Journal of Psychology*, *126*, 371-383.

Malouff, J., Schutte, N., Wiener, K., Brancazio, C. & Fish, D. (1993). Important characteristics of warning displays on alcohol containers. *Journal of Studies on Alcohol*, *54*, 457-461.

McKay, T. (2014, December 9). *One year after Uruguay legalized marijuana, here's what it has become*. Retrieved from http://mic.com/articles/106094/one-year-after-uruguay-legalized-marijuana-here-s-what-it-s-become.

Medical Marijuana. (2015). *Three states considering the legalization of medical marijuana*. Retrieved from http://medicalmarijuana.procon.org/view.esource.php?resourceID=002481.

New Health Guide. (2015). *Where is marijuana legal?* Retrieved from http://www.newhealthguide.org/Where-Is-Marijuana-Legal.html.

Pandey, A. (2015, July 25). Marijuana overdose through pot edibles a cause for concern, says CDC. *International Business News*. Retrieved from http://www.ibtimes.com/marijuana-overdose-through-pot-edibles-cause-concern-says-cdc-2025323.

Pfizer. (2013). *Medical information: Xanax*. Retrieved from https://www.pfizermedicalinformation.com/en-us/xanax.

Reilly, R. J. & Grim, R. (2013, August 30). Eric Holder says DOJ will let Washington, Colorado marijuana laws to into effect. *Huffington Post*. Retrieved from http://www.huffingtonpost.com.au/2013/08/29/eric-holder-marijuana-washington-colorado-doj_n_3837034.html?ir=Australia.

Rooke, S., Malouff, J. & Copeland, J. (2012). Effects of repeated exposure to a graphic smoking warning image. *Current Psychology*, *31*, 282-290.

Stout, D. & Moore, S. (2009, October 19). U.S. won't prosecute in states that allow medical marijuana. *New York Times*. Retrieved from http://www.nytimes.com/2009/10/20/us/20cannabis.html.

Stuart, H. & Wing, N. (2014, January 3). Here's why those 'marijuana deaths' don't change the debate on weed. *Huffington Post*. Retrieved from http://www.huffingtonpost.com.au/2014/02/28/marijuana-deaths_n_4868209.html?ir=Australia.

Tanquintic-Misa, E. (2015, March 20). Australians smoking less because of plain cigarette packaging. *International Business Times*. Retrieved from http://www.ibtimes.com.au/australians-smoking-less-because-plain-cigarette-packaging-1431500.

Tobacco Labelling Resource Centre. (2013). *Health warnings*. Retrieved from http://www.tobaccolabels.ca/healthwarningimages/.

U.S. Code of Federal Regulations. (2015). Alcoholic beverage health warning statement. 27 *United States Code* section 16.21.

U.S. Department of Health and Human Services. (1982). *The Surgeon General's warning on marijuana*. Retrieved from http://www.cdc.gov/mmwr/preview/mmwrhtml/00001143.htm.

Van Dam, N. T. & Earleywine, M. (2010). Pulmonary function in cannabis users: support for a clinical trial of the vaporizer. *International Journal of Drug Policy*, *21*, 511-513.

Volkow, N. D., Baler, R. D., Compton, W. M. & Weiss, S. R. (2014). Adverse health effects of marijuana use. *New England Journal of Medicine*, *370*, 2219-2227.

Wilkinson, C. & Room, R. (2009). Warnings on alcohol containers and advertisements: international experience and evidence on effects. *Drug and Alcohol Review*, *28*, 426-435.

World Health Organization. (2015). Health warning labels on alcohol containers: date by country. Retrieved from http://apps.who.int/gho/data/view.main.55920.

In: Marijuana
Editor: Margie Vasquez

ISBN: 978-1-63484-409-3

Chapter 6

Marijuana Regulation, Policy and Arrest Disparities: Their Impact on Recidivism and Negative Public and Mental Health Outcomes among African Americans

Torrance T. Stephens[1], PhD and Unity Harris[2]
[1]Department of Psychology and School of Education,
Clark Atlanta University, Atlanta, GA, US
[2]Department of Psychology, Clark
Atlanta University, Atlanta, GA, US

Abstract

The intent of this review is to exhibit how and the extent to which federal government marijuana regulation and policy contributes to disparities in arrest, in particular for African Americans of lower socioeconomic standing, thus leading to other negative outcomes including but not limited to poverty, health disparities, increased rates of sexually transmitted infections (STIs) and substance use and abuse. In this discussion, we will focus on the political history that has been institutionally imbued in the American politics and criminal justice system that increases the likelihood that African Americans, especially males, will be linked to stereotypical stigma that is a function of Western culture's socialization of men to accept norms that are not defined by the subjective experiences of African Americans. In conclusion, we proffer implications for perspective solutions to this problem including enhancing the quality of educational institutions and reducing educational failure in elementary and high schools, investments to enrich the quality of neighborhood environments and changes in policing and criminal justice policy that targets disproportionally African Americans, the poor and minorities.

INTRODUCTION

In the United States, the use of drugs and the promulgation of policies and legal manner in which drugs have been articulated and practiced has resulted in a disparate effect on poor and minority communities, in particular African Americans. This has been consistent historically ever since drugs and their uses have been targeted as both an immoral and as a form of criminal activity. With this in mind, the objective of this paper is to exhibit how and the extent to which federal government marijuana regulation and policy contributes to disparities in arrest, in particular for African Americans of lower socioeconomic standing, thus leading to other negative outcomes including but not limited to poverty, health disparities, increased rates of sexually transmitted infections (STIs) and substance use and abuse. In this discussion, we will focus on the political history that has been institutionally imbued in the American politics and criminal justice system that increases the likelihood that African Americans, especially males, will be linked to stereotypical stigma that is a function of Western culture's socialization of men to accept norms that are not defined by the subjective experiences of African Americans.

BRIEF HISTORY OF DRUG AND MARIJUANA REGULATION IN US

It is essential that the evaluation of Marijuana policy and regulation in the United States, as well as its impact on African Americans, that one must begin with an examination of drug policy in general in the United States and cultural views of minority communities in general. The consistency is that regardless of drugs targeted, policy always followed some relative pattern of implementation related to a selected target population.

The first overt example was opium. Historically in early America, opiates, just as cocaine, were often considered to be useful if not essential in everyday life in America (Musto, 1991). However, by the early 1900s, and well up until the start of the Second World War, the perception that these drugs were dangerous had increased and consequently policy accordingly to curtail this belief proffered. Strangely enough, the new policy regarding Opiates and cocaine was correlated with an increase of immigration of Asian and Latino populations. Historians have noted that well into the 19th century, drugs had been used in their natural form – especially Cocaine and morphine, for example, in the form of coca leaves or poppy plants that were chewed, or in some manner that diluted the impact of the active chemical compounds.

This time period was the start of the criminalization of substance use and it being correlated with ethnic parameters of the United States population and codified via law, the first being the 1909 "Act to Prohibit Importation and Use Of Opium and the Harrison Act of 1914 (Freericks, 1915; King, 1952; Musto, 1987). The "Act to Prohibit Importation and Use Of Opium was the first national legislation designed to regulate narcotics distribution and banned the importation of opium at specified ports and for other than medicinal use. It also required strict records regarding the importation of opium (Musto, 1972). More importantly, the original Harrison Act proffered penalties of no more than $2,000 in fines and/or more than five years imprisonment for violation of this law. However it's most profound impact was creating the image associated with one using opium, heroin or morphine as being a vagrant and immoral degenerate by imposing a stamp of illegitimacy on any unregulated narcotics use (King, 1952). Thus users were reduced to illegal and criminal means to purchase and procure these drugs. Criminal, because government regulation resulted in higher prices which frequently meant that users would often result to criminal behavior to be in a position to afford these drugs.

The clear outcome was a continuous cycle of behavior that served to reinforce the stereotype of the drug user via both the 1909 and 1914 laws: crimes were being committed so that addicts would be able to maintain a steady supply of opium-based drugs which fed into the histrionics and paranoia the public had been instructed to associate with the connection between criminal behavior and the use of opiates.

As a result of the Harrison Act, the public view of drug use and addictive behavior was redefined and states began to develop and create new legislation to deal with the drug problem which focused on punitive sanctions instead of treatment. This started with the Narcotics Division of the Prohibition Unit of the Internal Revenue Service created in 1920 and continued with the

Prohibition Bureau which was created in 1927 (Dickson, 1968; Meier, 1994). This has continued to be the accepted mainstream view of dealing with drug use until recent times (Collison, 1993; Humphreys, & Rappaport,1993; Fulton Hora, 2002).

Likewise when Mexican immigrants began to increase in number migrating to the United States, and unlike opium and cocaine, which was introduced during a period of tolerance regarding their use, marijuana was introduced the 1920s after the great depression and consequently associated with Hispanics and blacks. In fact the ethnic association of marijuana use became so connected to violence and criminal behavior during the height of the great depression during the 1930s that Mexican immigrants became more unwelcome minority and seen as a threat equally as blacks (Kaplan, Martin, Johnson, & Robbins, 1986; Musto, 1991). This was the culmination of prior national efforts to establish anti-marijuana legislation at the state and federal level and matched similar efforts in alcohol policy that had been implemented between 1900 and 1920 (Bonnie & Whitebread, 1970). For example, in 1914 and 1915 respectively, the New York City Sanitary Laws included cannabis in a prohibited drug list (Falck, 2002) and Utah passed the first state statute prohibiting sale or possession of the drug (Gieringer, 1999). Some fifteen years later, twenty-two states had similar laws on the books or pending legislation regarding marijuana (Bonnie & Whitebread, 1970).

The obvious result was the association between using marijuana, prior anti-narcotics and prohibition actions and it being considered as a criminal rather matter above all else. Finally In 1932, marijuana was included in the Uniform Narcotic Drug Act followed by the passage of the Marihuana Tax Act in 1937 (Musto, 1972). It has been suggested that these early laws not only codified the perception of the use of marijuana as a criminal activity but also the view that the lowest levels of American society were affiliated with its use tainted "by racial bias and sensationalistic myths" when smoking the plant was linked with violence (Bonnie & Whitebread, 1970).

From this time foreword, marijuana and policy regarding its cultivation, use and distribution has been observed notably as an issue for the criminal justice system, since most law enforcement officers and public officials support the contention that drug use is singularly a matter for the criminal justice system, and that punishment is the appropriate means to address this moral short coming via criminal sanction in an effort to encourage future abstinence and/or deterrence (Loue, 2003; Fentiman, 2011).

Marijuana Law, Policy and Arrest Disparities

Health disparities are defined by the According to the National Institutes of Health (2000) as differences in the incidence, prevalence, mortality, and burden of diseases and other adverse health conditions that exist among specific population groups in the United States." In the field of substance abuse, research shows that low-income African-Americans use drugs and alcohol at similar to or lower rates than Whites; however, low-income African-Americans experience significantly harsher consequences for their drug use and are less likely to engage in effective interventions (Schmidt, Greenfield, & Mulia, 2006; Windsor & Negi, 2009). For instance, when compared to Whites, African-Americans are more likely to have co-occurring disorders and die of cirrhosis of the liver (Caetano, 2003). Currently, African-Americans account for approximately half of new HIV infection cases in the United States. HIV-positive African-Americans die earlier than other racial groups due to barriers posed by poverty, lack of access to services, and avoidance of medical intervention due to medical mistrust and the stigma associated with HIV infection (Centers for Disease Control, 2007).

The phrase "war on drugs" was first used by President Nixon (Goode, 1997); however, what has manifested over the past thirty five years became popular under the administration of Ronald Reagan's as a part of his crime control strategy. During his tenure as President Reagan stated object was to direct attention towards reducing the drug supply by increasing resources for reducing drug demand and a vibrant public relations effort which included Nancy Reagan's "just say no" campaign. Regan increased federal spending during his tenure from 1.5 billion dollars in 1981 to 9.7 billion dollars by 1990 (Office of National Drug Control Policy, 1996). This also encompassed stringent interagency cooperation at the federal and subnational levels, inclusive of a 1978 forfeiture law (Myers and Brzostowski, 1982). In 1988 the Regan administration created the Office of National Drug Control Strategy and named William Bennett as its "drug czar."

After Reagan, President Bill Clinton built on his efforts namely by expanding the nation's perception that drugs and there use was the reason crime rates were increasing in America's urban areas. Consequently, through his being a Democrat who supported a firm anti-crime platform during his Presidential campaign, upon election he signed into law a comprehensive "Omnibus" crime bill containing anti-drug measures and even authorizing the imposition of the death penalty for certain federal drug-related offenses.

With Regan we saw the beginning of the impact this focus on criminalizing mainly economic and low level possession and/or economic drug activities, as of 1987, it was estimated that more than 75% of arrest across the nation regarding drug use and possession is due to marijuana (Bureau of Justice Statistics, 1988). Both Reagan and Clinton, using the Uniform Narcotic Drug Act and the creation of new policies to deal with drug use specifically targeting narcotics enforcement and for educating the public on drug problems resulted in a more prosecutorial approach to minor drug use and possession. And given that urban areas were of specific focus, results indicate that an overrepresentation of African Americans were incarcerated as compared to their numbers in the general population today (Hagan and Albonetti, 1982; Beckett and Western, 2001; Garland 2001; Wacquant 2001; Hawkins 2001; Kennedy 2001).

With this preoccupation with "being tough on crime, "many states spend more on incarceration than on higher education (Chambliss 1999). Moreover, from 1980 to 2000 the African American rate of incarceration has increased nearly threefold, making the disparity with White in terms of incarceration odds to an extreme of eight to one (Blumstein 2001) albeit roughly comprising 13% of the US population. Even more problematic is that African Americans, in particular males, comprise approximately half of all in jail or in prison across the nation (Bureau of Justice Statistics 2002).

This is well documented and confirmed by a report released by the Sentencing Project in 1990 noting that young men are even at greater risk of being incarcerated due to the justice system preoccupation with minor drug use. The reported indicated that nearly one in four black males in the 20-29 age groups was under some form of criminal justice supervision. However, since then there has been little if any change to address this disparity by policymakers, law enforcement and criminal justice specialist, although the one consistent is that policies ostensibly that target control crime and drug abuse tend to worsen the increasing racial disparity in the criminal justice system.

In New York for example, the "Stop-and-Frisk" program has been statistically demonstrated to disproportionately affected both African Americans (Spitzer, 1999) albeit, African Americans account for 26% of NYC's population but 51% of all stops (a significant disparity given that whites represent 43% of the population but only 13% of all stops (Eterno, 2001; Harcourt, 2001; McArdle and Erzen, 2001). To make the issue more impactful is that the NYPD specifically targets the use of marijuana in public view which has resulted in a record number of arrests for African Americans on marijuana charges (Flynn, 1998). This may be why some social scientist suggests that the US war on drugs had turned into a war on marijuana (King and Mauer, 2006). This observation is supported in areas outside of New York also. Using data collected during the 1980s and 1990s on of sentence severity identified and disparity by race and ethnicity, Spohn (2000) noted that almost half of the studies included in her meta-analysis showed on average, blacks received harsher sentences than whites regardless of sentence.

The aforementioned indicate that policing is a racially disparate action in itself and has resulted in severe and racially disparate consequences for African Americans regarding both criminal convictions and incarceration. In addition, since the 1990s, criminal justice policy regarding marijuana in the US became more harsh as reflected by limited judicial discretion in sentencing, "mandatory minimum sentences," and three-strike laws. This is complicated by efforts to treat adolescent offenders as adults under so-called "zero-tolerance" policies that have impacted Africa American communities, in particularly impoverished African American communities disproportionally (Kennedy, 2001; Williams & Collins, 2001; Golub, Johnson & Dunlap, 2007, Tonry & Melewski, 2008).

Marijuana Policy Public Health Impact on African Americans

It is clear that the result of policies and views regarding marijuana use has led to a dramatic and sizable increase in the number of people; especially African Americans, incarcerated jails and prisons. As a result, these policies have led to an increase of negative health outcomes manifesting at the individual and community. Freudenberg (2002) suggest that disproportionately high rates of incarceration in the African American community impacts heath negatively in several ways including placing individuals in environments with high rates of infectious and chronic diseases, reducing opportunities to required health services, breaking up families and separating women from their children, which increases all involved to be more at risk of psychological and mental health problems. Others have suggested that incarceration also effect families and individuals economically since, incarceration may result in one losing a job and income associated employment and possibly homelessness (Western, Kling & Weiman, 2001; Richie, 2001).

The irony is that these issues are created by policies that frequently proffer a greater burden economically for the nation than the problems they purport to address. Although the current rates of illicit drug use are roughly the same between Blacks and Whites (7.4% and 7.2%, respectively) White drug users comprise the majority of drug users, especially marijuana compared to African Americans because White people are a larger share of the population. Some researchers note that Whites and African Americans represent 72% and 15% respectively of all illicit drug users, with Whites being five times more likely than African Americans to use marijuana (Wu & Ringwalt, 2014; RTI International & United States of America, 2002).

In essence, instead of reducing the burden of the use of illicit substance like marijuana and reducing crime, current criminal justice policy creates crimes and a permanent criminal population that albeit statistically improbable, impact African Americans more than other racial ethnic parameters of the US population and more concerns to be addressed by public and mental health professional. Moore & Elkavich (2008) describes this as the "circular pattern" of incarceration and suggest that this creates a public health problem for which limited if any resources are established or in place "to address the consequences created by the imprisonment and subsequent life-altering progress of whole populations."

One example of the negative impact of incarceration on the health of Correctional policies contributes to disparities in health regards premature death. Empirical investigation supports that former prison inmates are at a statistically significant high risk for death after release from prison, particularly during the first 2 weeks (Binswanger, Stern, Deyo, et al., 2007). Some have contributed the higher premature death rates for inmates when compared to the general population to several factors which include problems that accompany the reentry process of reintegrating back into their community from incarceration, such as trying to obtain housing, secure employment, food and access to health care (Iguchi, London, Forge et al., 2002; Petersilia, 2003).

The overt understanding of what has been established is that marijuana is the most commonly abused illicit substance among all young adults (Aldworth, 2009) however, the research associating it's as a causative agent in criminal behavior is nebulous (Randall & Cunningham, 2003). This is the most obvious evidence of the negative impact incarceration has on the health of disparities among African Americans and proffers a public health rationale for policy change to reduce this health burden and the distorted re-incarceration rate of African American marijuana users.

African American male adolescents in particular, are incarcerated on drug use or sales charges disproportionate to their representation in the general population (Levine & Small, 2007; Freudenberg, Moseley, Labriola, et al., 2007) which are more a function of the failures of US educational practices (Ramchand, Morral & Becker, 2009) and psychological difficulties due to socioeconomic factors (Fazel, Doll & Långström, 2008; Lader, Singleton & Meltzer, 2003) more so than addiction and/or a predilection for criminal behavior. Unfortunately the result has been an increased risk for the contraction and spreading of sexually transmitted infections (STIs) such as higher rates of HIV when compared to non-jailed populations (Golzari, Hunt & Anoshiravani, 2006; Teplin, Elkington, McClelland & et al., 2005) This is complicated given that most adolescents are released from jail within a few weeks of arrest, usually without access to community services with a sizable majority being rearrested within a year (Fagan, 1996).

What must be understood for health professionals and professionals involved in the justice system is that Racial/ethnic differences in chronic morbidity and excess mortality are problematic in non-incarcerated communities and made even more pronounced among correctional populations. African Americans, in particular men, whom serve lengthy sentences in the criminal justice system, are even more impacted by negative health outcomes (Geronimus, 1991; Wong, Shapiro, Boscardin, & Ettner, 2002).

Some note that this is a result of the burden that stress experienced in living in a race-conscious society based on white supremacy that not only places non-whites at social disadvantages but also disproportionate impacts ones health in the form of morbidity and mortality. Thus African American men re-entering society after being incarcerated for whatever offence are to meaningful adapt, a stable living environment are needed for these men to be able to successfully reintegrate into both families and the larger society, and to avoid conditions that are precursors of health problems that may lead to future incarceration (Cooke, 2004).

IMPLICATIONS AND PERSPECTIVE FOR THE FUTURE

In closing, the health status of men is linked to the nature of social organization and of economic opportunity in society. This observation is no different for individuals with a history of incarceration – an incarceration contrived to fit social notions of vice and criminal behavior based on substance use, especially marijuana use. Consequently, improving the health of future generations of African Americans will require an honest and objective examination of the nature of the criminal justice system in terms of its disparate impact on communities that are targeted by laws based on unsubstantiated statistics and perceptions. It is well sustained that encounters with the police can be conditioned by prior attitudes about policing (Brandl, Frank, Worden, & Bynum, 1994; Rosenbaum, Schuck, Costello, et al., 2005).

It is also clear that improving the economic situations and educational opportunities of the African American community is essential if we are to break the biases associated with African Americans, drug use and law enforcement. In particular, based on the relationship between health outcomes and income inequality and the persistent lack of intergenerational wealth transferred at the family level among African Americans (Stephens, 2002). However, this must occur in concert with changes targeting the historical notion about the fundamental fairness of the criminal justice system and the systematic bias on the basis of race that may account for the large disparities African Americans experience within the criminal justice system.

The burden suffered by African Americas as an outcome of the war on drugs also impacts the general population. In 1995, it was estimated that the cost of incarceration for young African America males singularly was approximately $6 billion yearly (Mauer, & Huling, 1995).

A reasonable approximation given that 32.2% young African American males between the ages of 20 and 29 is under criminal justice supervision on any given day in the form of jail, probation, parole and/or prison (Davis, 2007) of which most being a consequence of drug policies that appear to have grown criminal justice populations in in state and federal prisons (Pettit, & Western, 2004). Similar trends are also reported for African American women whom incarceration rates in state prisons for drug offenses singularly in state prisons increasing more than 800% from 1986 to 1991 (Mauer, & Huling, 1995).

In closing, the most efficacious approach to addressing disparities in arrest due to the blanket criminalization of drug use and possession among African Americans is to focus on revising present policies from the local, state and federal level. This will require a reevaluation of how we define addiction and must make this a public health issue. It will also demand that we reform sentencing guidelines and direct spending toward enhancing the quality of educational institutions and reducing educational failure at the primary and secondary school level. Additional investments must focus on improving public and mental health outcomes that serve to enrich the quality of community and neighborhood environments. The aforementioned in conjunction with other efforts and programs aimed at transforming the structural barriers that disproportionately disadvantage at-risk African Americans (Brinkley-Rubinstein, Craven, & McCormack, 2014) are also paramount in altering the present landscape of drug policy and arrest disparities as a function of race and ethnicity. In the future, more studies such as this will foster empirically based assessments of the preventative needs of parameters of the African American at greatest risk of incarceration with respect to legal policy pertaining to marijuana use and its possession, and the role that race plays in risk of incarceration over time to try and highlight problems within the criminal justice system. Moreover, we must enhance social network relationships that may be negatively impacted by drug policy and sentencing with respect to the social experiences of discrimination that aggregate high-risk social ties in a network and explore the extent to which these affects serve as potential mechanism for racial/ethnic disparities outcomes.

Thus it is within our professional grasp to evaluate, understand and change problematic outcomes of disparities in incarceration based on race that impact individual and community mental and public health. It will require a systematic methodology based on public health policy set forth by our state and federal governments working in concert with communities and organizations at the neighborhood level.

REFERENCES

Aldworth, J. (2009). *Results from the 2007 national survey on drug use and health: National findings*. DIANE Publishing.

Beckett, Katherine and Bruce Western (2001). Governing social marginality: Welfare, incarceration, and the transformation of state policy. In: Garland (Ed.), *Mass Imprisonment: Social Causes and Consequences*. Thousand Oaks, CA: Sage Publications.

Binswanger, I. A., Stern, M. F., Deyo, R. A., Heagerty, P. J., Cheadle, A., Elmore, J. G. and Koepsell, T. D. (2007). Release from Prison — A High Risk of Death for Former Inmates. *The New England Journal of Medicine*, 356(2), 157–165. http://doi.org/10.1056/NEJMsa064115.

Blumstein, Alfred (2001). Race and criminal justice. In: Smelser, Wilson and Mitchell (Eds.), *America Becoming: Racial Trends and Their Consequences*, Volume II, pp. 21-31. Washington, DC: National Academy Press.

Bonnie, R. J. and Whitebread, C. H. (1970). The forbidden fruit and the tree of knowledge: an inquiry into the legal history of American marijuana prohibition. *Virginia Law Review*, 971-1203.

Bonnie, R. J. and Whitebread, C. H. (1974). The marihuana conviction: A history of marihuana prohibition in the United States. Charlottesville, VA: University Press of Virginia.

Brandl, S. G., Frank, J., Worden, R. E. and Bynum, T. S. (1994). Global and specific attitudes toward the police: Disentangling the relationship. *Justice Quarterly*, 11(1), 119-134.

Brinkley-Rubinstein, L., Craven, K. L. and McCormack, M. M. (2014). Shifting perceptions of race and incarceration as adolescents age: Addressing disproportionate minority contact by understanding how social environment informs racial attitudes. *Child and Adolescent Social Work Journal*, 31(1), 25-38.

Bureau of Justice Statistics. (1988). Bureau of Justice Statistics, 1987. Department of Justice, Washington, DC.

Bureau of Justice Statistics (2002). Correctional Populations in the United States 1998--Statistical Tables. (Publication No. NCJ 192929). Washington, DC.

Caetano, R. (2003). Alcohol-Related Health Disparities and Treatment-Related Epidemiological Findings Among Whites, Blacks, and Hispanics in the United States. *Alcoholism: Clinical and experimental research*, 27(8), 1337-1339. Centers for Disease Control. HIV/AIDS Surveillance Report. 2007. pp. 1-46. Retrieved from http://www.cdc.gov/hiv/topics/surveillance/resources/reports/2005report/pdf/2005SurveillanceReport.pdf.

Chambliss, William J (1999). Power, Politics, and Crime. Boulder, CO: Westview.

Collison, M. (1993). Punishing drugs criminal justice and drug use. *British Journal of Criminology*, 33(3), 382-399.

Cooke, C. L. (2004). Joblessness and homelessness as precursors of health problems in formerly incarcerated african american men. *Journal of Nursing Scholarship*, 36(2), 155-60. Retrieved from http://search.proquest.com/docview/236388267?accountid=4732.

Davis, A. (2007). Race and criminalization: Black Americans and the punishment industry. *Race, Ethnicity, and Gender Selected Readings*, 204-222.

Dickson, D. T. (1968). Bureaucracy and morality: An organizational perspective on a moral crusade. *Social Problems*, 16(2), 143-156.

Eterno, John A. Zero tolerance policing in democracies: The dilemma of controlling crime without increasing police abuse of power. *Police Practice*. 2001;2:189–217.

Fagan, J. (1996). The Comparative Advantage of Juvenile Versus Criminal Court Sanctions on Recidivism among Adolescent Felony Offenders*. *Law and Policy*, 18(1-2), 77-114.

Falck, Z. J. (2002). Controlling the weed nuisance in turn-of-the-century American cities. *Environmental history*, 611-631.

Fazel, S., Doll, H. and Långström, N. (2008). Mental disorders among adolescents in juvenile detention and correctional facilities: a systematic review and metaregression analysis of 25 surveys. *Journal of the American Academy of Child and Adolescent Psychiatry*, 47(9), 1010-1019.

Fentiman, L. C. (2011). Rethinking Addiction: Drugs, Deterrence, and the Neuroscience Revoltion. *U. Pa. JL and Soc. Change*, 14, 233.

Flynn Kevin. Arrests soar in crackdown on marijuana. *New York Times*. 1998 November 17:B-1.

Freericks, F. H. (1915). The harrison act. *Journal of the American Pharmaceutical Association*, 4(3), 397-405.

Freudenberg, N. (2002). Adverse Effects of US Jail and Prison Policies on the Health and Well-Being of Women of Color. *American Journal of Public Health*, 92(12), 1895-1899.

Freudenberg, N., Moseley, J., Labriola, M., Daniels, J. and Murrill, C. (2007). Comparison of health and social characteristics of people leaving New York City jails by age, gender, and race/ethnicity: implications for public health interventions. *Public Health Reports*, 122(6), 733.

Fulton Hora, H. P. (2002). A dozen years of drug treatment courts: Uncovering our theoretical foundation and the construction of a mainstream paradigm. *Substance Use and Misuse*, 37(12-13), 1469-1488.

Geronimus, A. T. (1991). The weathering hypothesis and the health of African-American women and infants: evidence and speculations. *Ethnicity and disease*, 2(3), 207-221.

Gieringer, D. H. (1999). The forgotten origins of cannabis prohibition in California. *Contemporary Drug Problems*, 26(2), 237-288.

Golub, A., Johnson, B. D. and Dunlap, E. (2007). The race/ethnicity disparity in misdemeanor marijuana arrests in New York City. *Criminology and public policy*, 6(1), 131.

Goode, E. (1997). Between Politics and Reason: The Drug Legalization Debate. New York: St. Martin's.

Gorman, D. M. (1993). War on drugs continues in United States under new leadership. *BMJ*, 307(6900), 369-371.

Golzari, M., Hunt, S. J. and Anoshiravani, A. (2006). The health status of youth in juvenile detention facilities. *Journal of Adolescent Health*, 38(6), 776-782.

Gray, J. (2010). Why our drug laws have failed: a judicial indictment of war on drugs. Temple University Press.

Hagan, John and C. Albonetti (1982) Race, class, and the perception of criminal injustice in America. *American Journal of Sociology*, 88: 329-355.

Harcourt Bernard E. Illusion of Order: The False Promise of Broken Windows Policing. Cambridge, Mass: Harvard; 2001.

Hawkins, Darnell F. (2001). Commentary on Randall Kennedy's overview of the justice system. In: Smelser, Wilson and Mitchell (Eds.), *America Becoming: Racial Trends and Their Consequences*, Volume II, pp. 32-51. Washington, DC: National Academy Press.

Humphreys, K. and Rappaport, J. (1993). From the community mental health movement to the war on drugs: A study in the definition of social problems. *American Psychologist*, 48(8), 892.

Iguchi, M. Y., London, J. A., Forge, N. G., Hickman, L., Fain, T. and Riehman, K. (2002). Elements of well-being affected by criminalizing the drug user. *Public Health Reports*, 117(Suppl. 1), S146.

Kaplan, H. B., Martin, S. S., Johnson, R. J. and Robbins, C. A. (1986). Escalation of marijuana use: Application of a general theory of deviant behavior. *Journal of health and social behavior*, 44-61.

Kennedy R. Racial trends in the administration of criminal justice. In: Smelser, N., Wilson, W. J., Mitchell, F., eds. *America Becoming: Racial Trends and Their Consequences*. Vol. 2. Washington, DC: National Academy Press; 2001:1-20.

King, R. G. (1952). Narcotics Bureau and the Harrison Act: Jailing the Healers and the Sick, The. Yale LJ, 62, 736.

King Ryan, S., Mauer Marc. The war on marijuana: The transformation of the war on drugs in the 1990s. *Harm Reduction Journal*. 2006 [Retrieved 09/ 16/15]. Available online: www.harmreductionjournal.com.

Lader, D., Singleton, N. and Meltzer, H. (2003). Psychiatric morbidity among young offenders in England and Wales. *International Review of Psychiatry*, 15(1-2), 144-147.

Levine, H. G. and Small, D. P. (2008). Marijuana Arrest Crusade: Racial Bias and Police Policy in New York City 1997-2007. New York Civil Liberties

Union. Levine, H. G. and Small, D. P. (2008). Marijuana Arrest Crusade: Racial Bias and Police Policy in New York City 1997-2007. New York Civil Liberties Union.

Loue, S. (2003). The criminalization of the addictions. *Journal of Legal Medicine*, 24(3), 281-330.

Mauer, M. and Huling, T. (1995). Young Black Americans and the Criminal Justice System: Five Years Later.

McArdle Andrea, Erzen Tanya, editors. Zero Tolerance: Quality of Life and the New Police Brutality in New York City. New York: New York University; 2001.

Meier, K. J. (1994). The politics of sin: Drugs, alcohol and public policy. ME Sharpe.

Moore, L. D. and Elkavich, A. (2008). Who's Using and Who's Doing Time: Incarceration, the War on Drugs, and Public Health. *American Journal of Public Health*, 98(5), 782-786. http://doi.org/10.2105/AJPH.2007.126284.

Morris, R. E., Baker, C. J., Valentine, M. and Pennisi, A. J. (1998). Variations in HIV risk behaviors of incarcerated juveniles during a four-year period: 1989-1992. *Journal of Adolescent Health*, 23(1), 39-48.

Musto, D. F. (1972). The marihuana tax act of 1937. *Archives of General Psychiatry*, 26(2), 101-108.

Musto, D. F. (1987). *The American disease: origins of narcotic control* (expanded edition). NY: Oxford.

Musto, D. F. (1991). Opium, cocaine and marijuana in American history. *Scientific American*, 265(1), 40-47.

Myers, H. L. and Brzostowski, J. P. (1982). Dealers, Dollars and Drugs: Law Enforcement's Promising New 3-Dimensional Program. *Drug Enforcement* 9 (1): 7-10.

National institutes of Health. (2009). Addressing health disparities: The NIH program of action.

Office of National Drug Policy. 1996. The National Drug Control Strategy, 1996: Program, Resources and Evaluation.

Petersilia, J. (2003). When prisoners come home: Parole and prisoner reentry. Oxford University Press.

Pettit, B. and Western, B. (2004). Mass imprisonment and the life course: Race and class inequality in US incarceration. *American Sociological Review*, 69(2), 151-169.

Ramchand, R., Morral, A. R. and Becker, K. (2009). Seven-year life outcomes of adolescent offenders in Los Angeles. *American Journal of Public Health*, 99(5), 863.

Randall, J. and Cunningham, P. B. (2003). Multisystemic therapy: A treatment for violent substance-abusing and substance-dependent juvenile offenders. *Addictive Behaviors*, 28(9), 1731-1739.

Richie, B. E. (2001). Challenges incarcerated women face as they return to their communities: Findings from life history interviews. *Crime and Delinquency*, 47(3), 368-389.

Rosenbaum, D. P., Schuck, A. M., Costello, S. K., Hawkins, D. F. and Ring, M. K. (2005). Attitudes toward the police: The effects of direct and vicarious experience. *Police quarterly*, 8(3), 343-365.

RTI International and United States of America. (2002). *Results From the 2001 National Household Survey on Drug Abuse*: Volume I. Summary of National Findings.

Schmidt, L., Greenfield, T. and Mulia, N. (2006). Unequal treatment: racial and ethnic disparities in alcoholism treatment services. *Alcohol Research and Health*, 29(1), 49.

Spohn Cassia C. Julie Horney, editor. Thirty years of sentencing reform: The quest for a racially neutral sentencing policy. *Criminal Justice 2000*. 2000 [Retrieved 02/03/06]. p. 3. Available online: www.ncjrs.gov.

Spitzer Eliot. The New York City Police Department's "Stop and Frisk" *Practices: A Report to the People of the State of New York from the Office of the Attorney General*. 1999 [Retrieved 02/07/06]. Available online: www.oag.state.ny.us.

Stephens, T. T. (2002). Conceptualizing Racial and Ethnic Disparities in Health in the Form of Intergenerational Transfer of Wealth. *Phylon* (1960-), 161-165.

Teplin, L. A., Elkington, K. S., McClelland, G. M., Abram, K. M., Mericle, A. A. and Washburn, J. J. (2014). Major mental disorders, substance use disorders, comorbidity, and HIV-AIDS risk behaviors in juvenile detainees. *Psychiatric Services*.

Tonry, M. and Melewski, M. (2008). The malign effects of drug and crime control policies on black Americans. *Crime and justice*, 37(1), 1-44.

Wacquant, L. (2001). Deadly symbiosis when ghetto and prison meet and mesh. *Punishment and Society*, 3(1), 95-133.

Western, B., Kling, J. R. and Weiman, D. F. (2001). The labor market consequences of incarceration. *Crime and delinquency*, 47(3), 410-427.

Wong, M. D., Shapiro, M. F., Boscardin, W. J. and Ettner, S. L. (2002). Contribution of major diseases to disparities in mortality. *New England Journal of Medicine*, 347(20), 1585-1592.

Windsor, L. C. and Negi, N. (2009). Substance abuse and dependence among low income African Americans: Using data from the National Survey on Drug Use and Health to demystify assumptions. *Journal of addictive diseases*, 28(3), 258-268.

Wu, L. T. and Ringwalt, C. (2014). Use of substance abuse services by young uninsured American adults. *Psychiatric Services and World Languages*.

In: Marijuana
Editor: Margie Vasquez

ISBN: 978-1-63484-409-3

Chapter 7

MARIJUANA AND VIDEO GAMES: "REAL" ADDICTIONS?

Geoffrey L. Ream*

School of Social Work, Adelphi University, Garden City, NY, US

What recreational marijuana use and entertainment video game play have in common is that they are benign much of the time, but they also have problem use patterns associated with them, and these problem use patterns are often misunderstood by both users and people concerned about them. One example of this misunderstanding is the question of whether marijuana and video games can engender "real" addictions. This commentary aims to answer this question in a way that bridges the gap between scientific and colloquial understandings of problem use, in hopes of helping service providers communicate effectively with users about whether they have a problem.

According to the International Classification of Disorders version 10 (ICD-10, World Health Organization, 1992) dependence on any substance (including marijuana) involves strong desire to take the substance, difficulty controlling use, a physiological withdrawal state, needing more of the substance for the same effect, prioritizing substance use over other activities, and persistence with use despite harmful consequences. Lifetime prevalence of cannabis dependence among Americans ages 24-32 in 2008-2009 was 8.3% (Haberstick et al., 2014). Many marijuana users also smoke tobacco and drink alcohol, and they may invoke the colloquial term "psychological addiction"

* E-mail address: ream@adelphi.edu.

(Newlin, 2008) to distinguish their experience with cannabis from the more intense alcohol and nicotine dependence syndromes which they know first-hand. Users of "blunts," which are cigar shells emptied out and filled with marijuana, tend to attribute their dependence symptoms to nicotine rather than cannabis (Dunlap, Benoit, Sifaneck, & Johnson, 2006). From a scientific perspective, these users are partially correct. There is a drug interaction between nicotine and cannabis that enhances cannabis' addictive properties and reduces its side-effects (Ream, Benoit, Johnson, & Dunlap, 2008). Users may experience cannabis as less addictive simply because it has less unpleasant withdrawal symptoms, owing to the fact that it remains in the body for a very long time. They may not realize that it is possible to experience other addiction symptoms, such as using in spite of detrimental consequences and having one's life revolve around use, to a great degree even without strong withdrawal symptoms.

In contrast to the situation with marijuana, there is no ICD-10 diagnosis for problem video game play. If ICD-10 criteria were to be created for video game addiction, they would probably be based on criteria for problem gambling, i.e., that the activity is financially unprofitable, attempts to quit or cut down have not worked, and it continues even though it causes personal distress and interferes with daily living (World Health Organization, 1992). Prevalence estimates of serious problem video game play range from 0.2% to 34% depending on the measure used and the population studied (Griffiths, Király, Pontes, & Demetrovics, 2015). Although neurological explanations for problem video game use revolve around the dopamine system, the video game genres most strongly associated with problem use are those that involve identification with a fictional character (Elliott, Ream, McGinsky, & Dunlap, 2012). There is not yet a clear, direct biological explanation for why this should be. In one study, users' own perspectives on video game addiction focused on one specific genre that involves identification with a fictional character: Massively Multiplayer Online Role-Playing Games (Elliott, Ream, & McGinsky, 2012). This study may have captured a cross-section of a larger trend of video game players becoming strongly engaged with – and, therefore, more often developing problem use of – whichever games are/were most popular during their peak video gaming years (Ream, Elliott, & Dunlap, 2013a). Players' and scientists' perspectives tend to be in agreement that only a fraction of people who are heavily engaged with video games are actually problem users, that video game play ought to (and usually does) diminish when life obligations interfere with it, and that someone can be said to have a problem when video gaming diverts them from adult responsibilities (Elliott, Ream, McGinsky, et al., 2012; Ream, Elliott, & Dunlap, 2013b).

Concurrent use of video games and substances is not uncommon. People who do this recognize that video games may enhance the positive experience of substance use and vice versa, and also that video games and substances may remediate each other's undesirable effects. Examples of this include drinking caffeine to enhance video game performance, smoking marijuana to calm down after a "rage quit," or playing video games to pass time while hung over. Concurrent users may play video games to pass time while experiencing the effects of substances or engage in concurrent use of video games and substances to cope with loneliness or depression (Ream, Elliott, & Dunlap, 2011a). Although users are self-aware of these motives for concurrent use of video games and substances, what they might not realize is that concurrent use of video games with substances, including marijuana, is associated with stronger substance dependence symptoms (Ream, Elliott, & Dunlap, 2011b).

Ultimately, the answer to whether marijuana use or video game play can lead to "real" addictions is that yes, this is possible, depending on specifics of the individual's use and how it fits into the rest of their lives. It would be easy to say that educational use of video games and clinical use of marijuana are benign while entertainment use of video games and recreational use of marijuana could lead to problems, but this statement would be more ideological than scientific. Research has not affirmed that educational use of video games and clinical use of marijuana cannot lead to problem use. Moreover, entertainment use of video games and recreational use of marijuana could be for benign reasons. People use marijuana to help extinguish aversive memories, reduce depression, and reduce nicotine withdrawal symptoms because it works (Ream et al., 2008), and video game players see even addiction-like video game use as still less problematic than many other things that they could be doing with their free time (Elliott, Ream, McGinsky, et al., 2012). It would not even be appropriate to say that someone getting into legal trouble over marijuana necessarily has a problem, because likelihood of police stop/search or arrest for marijuana has far more to do with a user's race, gender, and which part of town they are in than any aspect of their use (Ream, Johnson, Dunlap, & Benoit, 2010). There are also social misuses of the concept of problem use, such as the legal system diverting youth guilty for marijuana offenses into drug treatment that they do not need, or medical providers (at least giving the impression of) considering a child's long hours spent playing video games as evidence of attention-deficit or bipolar disorder. Assessment of problem use must always address the central question of whether someone is experiencing a behavioral compulsion that is causing them distress and/or getting in the way of what they want/need to (and realistically could be) doing with their lives. This is the appropriate benchmark for "real" addiction.

Acknowledgments

Special thanks to Jesse Penber for help with manuscript development.

References

Dunlap, E., Benoit, E., Sifaneck, S. J., & Johnson, B. D. (2006). Social constructions of dependency by blunts smokers: Qualitative reports. *International Journal of Drug Policy, 17*(3), 171-182. doi:10.1016/j.drugpo.2006.01.004.

Elliott, L. C., Ream, G. L., & McGinsky, E. (2012). Video game addiction: User perspectives. In J. Netherland (Ed.), *Critical Perspectives on Addiction* (pp. 225-243). Bingley, UK: Emerald Group Publishing Limited.

Elliott, L. C., Ream, G. L., McGinsky, E., & Dunlap, E. (2012). The contribution of game genre and other use patterns to Problem Video Game Play among adult video gamers. *International Journal of Mental Health and Addiction, 10*(6), 948-969. doi:10.1007/s11469-012-9391-4.

Griffiths, M. D., Király, O., Pontes, H. M., & Demetrovics, Z. (2015). An overview of problematic gaming. In E. Aboujaoude & V. Starcevic (Eds.), *Mental health in the digital age: Grave dangers, great promise* (pp. 27-45). New York, NY, US: Oxford University Press.

Haberstick, B. C., Young, S. E., Zeiger, J. S., Lessem, J. M., Hewitt, J. K., & Hopfer, C. J. (2014). Prevalence and correlates of alcohol and cannabis use disorders in the United States: Results from the National Longitudinal Study of Adolescent Health. *Drug and Alcohol Dependence, 136*, 158-161. doi:http://dx.doi.org/10.1016/j.drugalcdep.2013.11.022.

Newlin, D. B. (2008). Are "physiological" and "psychological" addiction really different? Well, no!... um, er, yes? *Substance use & misuse, 43*(7), 967-971. doi:10.1080/10826080802097389.

Ream, G. L., Benoit, E., Johnson, B. D., & Dunlap, E. (2008). Smoking tobacco along with marijuana increases symptoms of cannabis dependence. *Drug and Alcohol Dependence, 95*(3), 199-208. doi:10.1016/j.drugalcdep.2008.01.011.

Ream, G. L., Elliott, L. C., & Dunlap, E. (2011a). Patterns of and motivations for concurrent use of video games and substances. *International Journal of Environmental Research and Public Health, 8*(10), 3999-4012. doi:10.3390/ijerph8103999.

Ream, G. L., Elliott, L. C., & Dunlap, E. (2011b). Playing video games while using or feeling the effects of substances: Associations with substance use problems. *International Journal of Environmental Research and Public Health, 8*(10), 3979-3998. doi:10.3390/ijerph8103979.

Ream, G. L., Elliott, L. C., & Dunlap, E. (2013a). A genre-specific investigation of predictors of video game engagement and problem play in the early life course. *Journal of Addiction Research & Therapy, S6*(Special Issue: Substance and Behavioral Addictions, edited by Kuss, D. J.). http://www.omicsonline.org/2155-6105/2155-6105-S6-008.php?aid=14564 doi:10.4172/2155-6105.S6-008.

Ream, G. L., Elliott, L. C., & Dunlap, E. (2013b). Trends in video game play through childhood, adolescence, and emerging adulthood. *Psychiatry Journal.* http://www.hindawi.com/journals/psyj/aip/301460/doi:10.1155/2013/301460.

Ream, G. L., Johnson, B. D., Dunlap, E., & Benoit, E. (2010). The role of marijuana use etiquette in avoiding targeted police enforcement. *Drugs: Education, Prevention & Policy, 17*(6), 689-706. doi:10.3109/096876309 02817993.

World Health Organization. (1992). The ICD-10 Classification of Mental and Behavioural Disorders: Diagnostic criteria for research. Retrieved from http://www.who.int/classifications/icd/en/GRNBOOK.pdf.

INDEX